DEMYSTIFYING AND DIGNIFYING SINGLEHOOD

DEMYSTIFYING AND DIGNIFYING SINGLEHOOD

Life Journeys of Single Women Across the Globe

Uma Jain

Crafting pathways *on rough* terrains

First published in 2023 by the NTL Institute
NTL Institute is an imprint of Libri Publishing

Copyright © Uma Jain

The right of Uma Jain to be identified as the author of this work has been asserted in accordance with the Copyright, Designs and Patents Act, 1988.

The author is a member of NTL Institute for Applied Behavioral Science. Views expressed are those of the author and contributors alone.

ISBN: 978-1-911451-13-6

All rights reserved.

A CIP catalogue record for this book is available from The British Library

Libri Publishing
Brunel House
Volunteer Way
Faringdon
Oxfordshire
SN7 7YR

Tel: +44 (0)845 873 3837

www.libripublishing.co.uk

Contents

Preface ix

Acknowledgements xiii

Introduction: Illuminating Rising Singlehood and Societal Narratives 1

1. Choices, Consequences, and Meaning-making: Living My Values and Truth 11
   Uma Jain, India

2. Single: Another (Way to Be) Other 37
   Heather Berthoud, USA

3. Happily Single 47
   Shobha Sarma, India

4. Why I Chose to Remain Single: To Get Freedom *from*, Freedom *to*, or *Inner* Freedom? 63
   S. Uma Devi, India

5. My Journey Towards Wholeness, as a Single Woman 81
   Julian Walker, UK

6. Single Woman in a Men's World 95
   Anney George, India

7.	My Non-traditional Journey *Deborah Howard, USA*	109
8.	My Life's Shades and Colours... *Archana Shrivastava, India*	119
9.	In Pursuit of Learning and Freedom *Vidya Gupta, India*	133
10.	An Unexpected and (Mostly) Happy State of Being *Sharon L. Miller, USA*	145
11.	The Tortoise on the Road *Rita Aggarwal, India*	151
12.	Destiny Created the Choice *Anjali Khanna, India*	163
13.	Reclaiming Myself – Realising My Dreams *Tangil Smith, USA*	171
14.	Becoming Whole... Singly *Priya Vasudevan, India*	185
15.	Of Freedom and Fairy Tales *Mukta Kamplikar, India*	195
16.	Single Women Lives: Significant Themes and Patterns *Uma Jain*	213
17.	Epilogue: Learnings and Vision for the Future: A World Thriving with Diversity *Uma Jain*	231

About the Contributors	239
About Dr. Uma Jain	245

This strange generation exists between sleeping and waking. It holds in its hands the soil of the past and the seeds of the future. However, we find in every city a woman who symbolizes the future.

Khalil Gibran[1]

---

[1] Khalil Gibran, *The Greatest Works of Khalil Gibran* (Bombay: Jaico Publishing House, 1988), p. 399.

Preface

This book attempts to demystify and dignify singlehood. It presents the life journeys of single women as they walk on the rough terrains of singlehood, crafting new pathways. Single women share their experiences, relationships, life choices, pains and joys, gains and losses, and their ongoing learning.

Writing about single women lives has been my dream for over a decade. It initially began as an idea to write my own story. Not because I was keen, or found it easy, to write about my life – I was somewhat ambivalent about publishing a personal story and delayed it for years. But I believed I had a significant perspective to share with society for filling a gap in knowledge. So much in my life seemed different; sometimes, it felt unique in a positive way; sometimes difficult, and occasionally strange (or even odd) compared to the 'normal model' of a woman's life. It seemed more like the life of an outsider in society. While I believed my life was interrelated with society's norms and processes, I had kept my inner world to myself. I also believed there was so much richness in my experiences to learn from – for women, men, and society in general. I felt that I owed it to society and to myself to share my story at this stage of my sojourn on this earth. Later, this thought evolved into the idea of involving other single women, who had their own unique stories to share, with the hope that it would lead to some learning for us and society.

PREFACE

I started working on convening a single (never married) women's gathering for us to share and write our life journeys. During one writers' retreat in France in 2017, I shared this plan with two women colleagues and friends from the USA who identified themselves as single – Heather Berthoud and Deborah Howard. They joined me to make the single women's gathering happen. We broadened the definition of singlehood to also include women who believe that they have lived a significant part of their life in singlehood whether due to separation, divorce, or death of their spouse. This gathering took place in Jaipur, India, in 2018 with 15 single women from India and the USA. The experience and the learnings from it validated the need for this book. Some of the contributors to this book had not attended the gathering, but most of the women I invited to write affirmed the need, and gladly agreed to participate. Hence the idea has come to life.

In the current world, there are a significant and growing number of other people besides single women, with social identities which do not fit into the dominant narratives and gender constructs of society. Some of them are lesbian, gay, transgender, and people with chosen gender identities different from their biological sex. Paradoxically, however, neither the dominant narratives of society have changed nor the inevitable consequences that follow for these people, impacting the quality of their human experience.

I focus on the lives of women who live outside the dominant paradigm of marriage. I have chosen this focus as, having access to my own experiences in life as a single woman and those of the other women I have known over several decades, I believe that I have something significant to contribute. I acknowledge that this means not highlighting the unique issues of other non-dominant social identities. However, I believe that at least a good part of these experiences will be shared by others who live outside the dominant paradigm of heterosexual marriage.

Awareness about and visibility of some of the identities that live beyond the restrictions of societal culture's traditional binary gender construct have grown in recent decades. Singlehood is less understood and often takes on a view that it is a happening caused by the person's actions independent of societal culture, and needs to be corrected. There is a sense of mystery around the lives of single women. They do not fall into the dominant societal narratives of women's lives, such as the daughter-in-law, wife, mother, grandmother or a nurturing homemaker. Hence, they become the subject of uncomfortable and *undignifying* curiosity, assumptions, judgements, and projections. As I reviewed the writings available on the lives of single women, two themes emerged: single women, or people writing about them, elucidating their plight, asking society to do something to protect and support single women; or glamourising being single as a chosen utopian life, as if they have figured it all out. Some of them focus on one particular cause or outcome of being single. This book stands apart.

The purpose of this book is to bridge a gap in the social narratives by sharing life journeys of single women, through their authentic statements about their lives, to demystify and dignify singlehood and illuminate its relationship with societal culture. I envision this as an effort towards a wholesome life for diverse people on this planet which includes being known, understood, and accepted for who they are rather than put into stereotypes or excluded.

I have worked with single women for around three years for this book, to delve deeper and unearth their journeys about the causes and experiences of being single. A good number of the writers in this book are from the human development profession and speak their truth with awareness and openness in the service of learning. My four decades of work as an applied behavioural science professional and my long-standing relationship with several of the authors made it an exciting venture of re-living our journeys, learning about ourselves in depth, in the process of writing our truth. I have edited the journey versions many times, working with the authors to encourage and support them in articulating their truth with depth, focus, and authenticity.

All contributors were to write with the same set of questions in mind, to focus on the overall purpose and context of this work. Each writer, however, has her own style and a special story that unfolds in different ways, as the ways of constructing the world, experiencing, and expressing are different for different people. As an editor, I have retained the unique flavour, taste, and form of the stories. These writings might not always read like sophisticated literary writing. Neither will they present dramatically sad or happy endings, romantic descriptions, easy to-do lists, or consistent conclusions, which some readers might like. I hope the readers will enjoy the differences and levels of experience.

I am happy to bring this book out with the belief and hope that these journeys will touch the lives of single women wanting to create a new path for themselves and others who are not served well by society's dominant narratives. As the societal cultures are struggling to loosen the restrictions of the gender constructs, hopefully, these journeys will show new pathways on various unexplored terrains. I also believe that we can reconstruct and reshape the dominant narratives by making our ongoing stories public, building collective awareness.

Acknowledgements

It was a solo journey as a writer and editor to retain trust in the purpose of this work, as it does not fall into either academic or popular interests of people. I could have completed a venture like this over the last four years only with the support, help, and encouragement of like-minded people who see its value for themselves and society. I want to mention some of them. I am grateful to all the writers who took time and courage to write, going through several reviews and revisions. Heather Berthoud and Deborah Howard played a special role and worked with me for the single women workshop, which provided momentum to this project. Deborah Howard reviewed the journeys I had edited and gave many valuable comments and suggestions for further refinement. Some other friends and contributors on whom I continually drew as a sounding board and for reviewing my chapters were Archana Shrivastava and Mukta Kamplikar. My friend Ganesh Anantharaman reviewed my drafts and helped me sustain my faith and interest. My friend and wise senior professional Alexandra Merrill reviewed some chapters and gave comments from her unique perspective on gender and sexual identities. I am immensely grateful to all of those mentioned as well as many more friends, colleagues, and acquaintances who supported me in completing this self-assigned project. Lastly but significantly, I am grateful to Yvette A. Hyater-Adams for her expert critiquing, suggestions, and meticulous editing of my manuscript, particularly working with me closely to refine and enrich my chapters.

*****

> We're not yet
> where we're going;
> but we're not still
> where we were.
>
> Natasha Josefowitz[2]

---

[2] Natasha Josefowitz, *Is this where I was going?* (USA: Warner Communications, 1980), p. 109.

Introduction: Illuminating Rising Singlehood and Societal Narratives

When I was growing up, getting married was an assumed choice back in the 1960s. Women (called girls) had to be somehow attractive enough to be selected by a man (called a boy). This could mean upgrading one's capacities to earn for supplementing a future husband's income or making oneself desirable as per societal expectations – for example, by being a good cook, hiding a dark skin colour or spectacles, wearing makeup to look fair and beautiful, or wearing heels to look taller. It could even mean downsizing and downgrading oneself, dampening one's potential – for example, not going for higher studies, being willing to give up a promising career, and settling for an easier job to be a good housewife. Also, it could mean not expressing views (which, as per one's elders, meant talking too much, which would make it difficult to find a match).

However, amid this milieu, some young women began to make different choices, and I was one of them. There were very few such women visibly around at that time. Today, about 60 years later, there are many – millions of them. Also, millions of marriages are ending in divorce, but still the frequently asked question – and even if unasked, the one in people's minds – for single women is, "Why didn't you get married?" A highly surprised, sometimes even shocked look, is visible when someone learns that a woman above a certain apparent age is not married. Since the assumption is that everyone is married and has children, sometimes the first question is, "How many children do you have?" The rest follows. Many questions, assumptions, projections, and words of advice land upon single women, perhaps coming from curiosity, disapproval, sympathy or even pity, envy, and a whole host of other feelings generated in people due to their singlehood. Is it not worth reflecting on why married people are not asked, "Why did you get married or still continue in your marriage?" Or "Why do you have children?" Most likely because being married is assumed to be normal whereas being single is seen as an individual oddity rather than something intertwined with the many choices of so-called 'normal' people in society.

People make choices about their lives, even if by default, and are responsible for them. However, we need to move beyond this premise about this rising phenomenon. Men in society hold economic and institutional power, enacted and demonstrated in male supremacy. For example, men often control where and how much the woman will work and how the money she earns will be used. Women are expected to take the major responsibility on the home front. They either end up working too hard to meet all expectations, or compromising on the professional front, giving less than their best performance. Does all this not result in some women remaining single and focusing primarily on a career? Dowry expectations in some cultures, incompatible partnerships, lack of respect, freedom, choice, and love in marriage, being used as a physical object, could these not cause many divorces and women choosing to remain single? But often, this is not given a thought, and single woman becomes the target in society.

Based on my own experience and the stories of many women I have met, including the life journeys in this book, I have come to understand and believe that the rising singlehood phenomenon and its experience closely interlink with society. There is a simultaneous presence of the deep-rooted traditional societal cultures of patriarchy, sexism, and heterosexism* to a lesser or higher degree in most societies, along with the changes brought about by forces of modernisation. The play of these contradictory forces presents unprecedented complexity for women, making it imperative and possible for many women to choose to be single. At the same time, these very forces create and perpetuate the isolation and social injustice in single women's lives, as they are often judged from the lenses of traditional cultures. Marriage is still a valued status and often unnoticed and unacknowledged privileges – emotional, social, and material – follow, while being single comes at a price for living outside society's dominant narratives. I elaborate on my hypotheses further, and the life journeys in this book will illustrate many dimensions of these dynamics.

Industrialisation, modernisation, and social reform movements in the nineteenth century have resulted in women's awareness, education, and employment in economic activities outside their homes. Education and financial independence have raised their aspirations about career, life, and the nature of marital relationships. There is simultaneity of the stagnant societal narratives about women's lives and the changes in awareness and economic status. It operates at many levels in society – in men, families, social systems, and not insignificantly within and amongst women who are subjected to contrary beliefs, assumptions, and their consequences. Often, due to the compulsions of economic needs or a desire for material enhancement, it is accepted and even wanted that women leave home for work, but they are still expected to maintain the traditional cultural norms of behaviour. This expectation is within themselves, family members, other people they encounter, and within the systems they enter. The coexistence of traditional and new role expectations creates a complex, challenging, and burdensome situation for women, pushing them towards 'either/or' options. Chapter 16 in the book elaborates on how various factors play a role in the choice or outcome of singlehood.

---

* Terms marked with an asterisk are defined at the end of this introduction.

There might be a temptation to quote exceptional contrary examples of women who appear to have successfully combined marriage with exemplary achievements, but the phenomenon I narrate above is widely prevalent. I invite the readers to notice this intricate dance as a social observer, thinker, and social being – as a continuing receiver of the consequences of this dance. Narratives of women in this book demystify how this complex, artful design of traditional and emerging societal cultures weaves through the minds, feelings, and actions of the actors involved in the stories of many women in different forms. They demonstrate how social structures, cultures, and systems make it extremely difficult for women to lead a wholesome life of their choice, leading to an increasing number taking the option of being single.

Through this book, I ask society – people and institutions – to notice and reflect on the traditional cultural processes of patriarchy, sexism, misogyny, heterosexism, and marriageism* at play and their intersectionality intensifying the complexity. Some readers might ask, given that these have existed for centuries, why is singlehood on the increase now? Marriage is no longer a dire economic necessity for many women in the way it used to be, as work opportunities for women outside homes have enlarged in the last several decades. An increasing number of women want, are able, and choose to be single to live a life of freedom, dignity, and meaningful professional accomplishments even if it means living outside of the lifestyles acceptable to society.

It is not surprising, then, that the population of single women around the world is now large and growing, leading to the emergence of singlehood as a way of life for women. For some, singlehood has meant never marrying; some chose it after a dysfunctional marriage or widowhood destined by fate. However, singlehood is still perceived as an aberration – often treated as an abnormality or sub-normality rather than a normal difference – particularly for a woman. Society continues to engage in othering single women. Single status is even turned into their primary identity, leading to marginalisation and exclusion, not just occasionally but as a regular pattern. Societies or cultures cannot keep shutting their eyes and operate on assumptions and myths, but need to know the lives of single women and how they are impacted by society, and in turn, how they impact it.

Life journeys of 15 women from India, the United States, and Europe are included in this book. These women are special and not invisible, unlike the often-imagined picture of single women. They have made significant accomplishments in varied professions including academia, journalism, the social sector, Vedanta teaching, counselling, human resources, training, and Organisation Development, leading lives different from the dominant narratives of society. While their contributions are often taken for granted, they miss some of the comforts, privileges, acceptance, and support often associated with being in the dominant narrative. These single women create new alternatives for strength, support, capacity, and meaning in their lives, adding value to the professional and social spaces they are in.

The narratives presented elucidate that single women often walk through the rough path of aloneness, invisibility, exclusion, and indignity towards self-respect, dignity, integration, and connection. The journeys show how they hold their past, present, and future with courage, hope, freedom, independence, and a sense of fullness and meaning, even in the midst of feeling alone and isolated. They elucidate the dance of singlehood as they embrace the pain and joy, tears and laughter, solitude and togetherness that come their way on the path they have chosen. It is about the struggle of women to be, to live, and to actualise their true selves.

While each journey is unique at one level – special events, circumstances, personality differences, and various other factors leading them to be single – there are also patterns and commonalities amongst them. Interestingly, even in women's experiences across nationalities, though content and events may sometimes seem different, many of the patterns and processes are similar, and the dominant narrative about women's lives has not changed.

INTRODUCTION

The purpose of sharing these stories is neither to seek sympathy, nor to criticise men, families, or society, but to contribute to bridging a gap in knowledge about the lives of people who live outside the dominant narratives of society, for collective learning. It is also not about presenting a utopian or rosy picture of singlehood to glamourise or propagate it, but rather enhancing awareness amongst all about various sides of the single women lives, the patterns, their reasons, and their interconnectedness with society.

Another way to understand this book is that these are stories of some women in transitional societies who tread a different path by choice and/or circumstances, and who show the path for change. Through the increasing emergence of single women as living examples, society demonstrates awareness about the *unviability* of its current systems and processes, which thrive on burdening women and even men to live up to the traditions amid changing social and economic scenarios. Married women also contribute to the process of setting up some women to be single by sharing the pains they experience in their marriages privately or offering unsolicited approval to the choice of singlehood as advisors, while their own choices perpetuate the status quo. Perhaps they express their rebellion or ambivalence towards the institution of marriage through other women but are unwilling to pay the price themselves. Society continues to maintain the status quo by excluding single women as the other and an oddity.

The first 15 chapters contain individual journeys. Names in the journeys are the contributors' actual names, except where it is stated otherwise. Chapter 16 gives patterns and themes that I have culled from these journeys, some more data from workshops I conducted, and my conversations with many other single women. These paint an emerging picture of a single woman's life. Ideally, reading these themes after reading complete individual journeys and delving into their uniqueness will be the best use of the book. Chapter 17 presents some of my learnings, dreams, and vision for single women and others who do not identify with the dominant narratives of society, as well as for partnered women, men, and society.

I believe a variety of readers will find meaning in these stories. Single women will find a connection with their own stories; single men too will find themes that touch their lives. Spouses of women may find out what makes wives leave marriages and what can make a marriage more meaningful and lasting. Parents of daughters may understand their daughters better. And other people who are curious to understand the steady increase in the social phenomenon of singlehood may find it informative.

These journeys will touch the lives of everyone in society in some way – as deep inside, even living amid the dominant narrative, there may be an experience of being different, alone, not belonging, and in a way, of singlehood. These women chose to listen to themselves and speak their truth, which many of us may not even acknowledge, taking the dominant narrative as the only reality.

*****

Terminology and Definitions

Patriarchy: *Broadly,* control by men of a disproportionately large share of power.
Retrieved 11 November 2022. Source: https://www.merriam-webster.com/dictionary/patriarchy

Misogyny: Hatred of, aversion to, or prejudice against women.
Retrieved 11 November 2022. Source: https://www.merriam-webster.com/dictionary/misogyny

Sexism: Prejudice or discrimination based on sex especially: discrimination against women.
Retrieved 11 November 2022. Source: https://www.merriam-webster.com/dictionary/sexism

Heterosexism: Discrimination or prejudice against non-heterosexual people based on the belief that heterosexuality is the only normal and natural expression of sexuality.
Retrieved 11 November 2022. Source: https://www.merriam-webster.com/dictionary/heterosexism

Marriageism: Though not found in the dictionary, this term is now being used by some people (and in this book) to refer to a social belief system which considers married status as superior to single or unmarried status.

We are
Today's women
Born yesterday
Dealing with tomorrow.

Natasha Josefowitz[1]

---

[1] Josefowitz, op. cit., 1980, p. 4.

Choices, Consequences, and Meaning-making: Living My Values and Truth

Uma Jain, India

> The heart of man is very much like the sea, it has its storms, it has its tides and in its depths it has its pearls too.
>
> Vincent van Gogh[1]

These words of van Gogh speak to me and connect to my life, as well as the life journeys of many single women. I only wish he had said "The heart of human beings" and not "of man." I would like to presume he meant that though, given the times in which he said it. In this narrative, I give a glimpse of the depth and range of my experiences in my life journey with the storms, tides, and pearls – the challenges, pains, sense of fulfilment, and joy from the choices I made. I also share my reflections, learnings, and the meaning I make of them. I speak my truth and the story I have lived and constructed in my awareness from the time the foundations of my singlehood began to be laid – brick by brick.

---

1 Vincent van Gogh, *The Letters of Vincent van Gogh*. Retrieved 19 November 2022. Source: https://www.goodreads.com/quotes/805924-the-heart-of-man-is-very-much-like-the-sea

Foundations of Singlehood

This journey into singlehood began perhaps even before I was born. It was conceived in the family and collective unconscious of society enacted through my parents, teachers, and other elders around me. Seeds of being single were sown, and the preparation for it began early in my life.

Undermining of My Feminine Self

Born as the sixth child and fourth daughter of a middle-class family, when I was very young I remember hearing my mother talking to some guests, sharing her unfulfilled hope of having a son after three daughters in a row. So, I picked up the message that my birth as a girl child was a disappointment for my parents.

In some ways, I felt neglected by my parents – maybe because of having six siblings – but in other ways, I felt treated as special by my father, teachers, and elder brothers. They carried high expectations of me: that I not become like the normal run of girls at that time – interested in clothes, jewellery, getting married, and the various leisure activities girls engage in, tantamount to being like a boy or maybe a goddess. Instilled into me was the message that I was supposed to be different, more than, better than, and not just one of the many children. In his brief interactions with me, my father used to inspire me to make exemplary achievements. One day he even said, "You should be like Vijay Lakshmi Pandit" (a famous woman intellectual). He expected me to set standards of behaviour and live a lifestyle that was different from my sisters. I began to make every effort to fulfil these expectations and at least not be a bother – as I was already one, being a girl.

My teachers saw me as a brilliant student. I remember that when I was in the sixth standard, one of them said to me, after I'd been absent from school for a day, "you should not be absent as I don't like to teach when you are not there." Such incidents meant a lot to me and probably compensated for the lack of significance and visibility I often experienced at home. I also demonstrated talents in extracurricular activities. School became the focus of my life, rather than leisure pursuits. When I did indulge in leisure activities occasionally, I felt rather guilty. I was afraid of lowering the possibility of my academic success and hence losing the little visibility and significance that I enjoyed in life through that. I felt as if I existed only if I were different or better than others. I realised only later that unconsciously, as a girl, I felt unwanted, and I had to prove my worthiness again and again.

I was not clear about what better really means – standing first in the class or excelling in extracurricular activities, or not being interested in what most girls like. I also convinced myself that joining family get-togethers or outings was not worth it. I began to believe that I would be good enough and able to survive in this world only by spending all my time in studies or other purposeful activities, staying away from leisure pursuits. I could not imagine, though, the price I would pay in the process of becoming special and high performing.

I was also highly sensitive to others' opinions, wanting to be perfect and not do anything wrong, to avoid criticism or reprimand. I felt pressured by the expectations for performance and restricted by the injunctions of my parents and elders with no sense of freedom and security to be myself. However, I did not feel protected so that I might trust that my needs would be taken care of by them. Hence, I developed a strong stance – of being aloof, unapproachable, and self-sufficient with the goal of becoming economically independent.

These experiences, stances, and choices meant the undermining of my feminine self and undoubtedly were not preparing me for marriage in my social context, thus strengthening the foundation of singlehood.

Two Stories – Inner and Outer

In addition to the part of me that stood strong, there was also a part within me that was a tender, vulnerable girl full of wishes and fantasies. So, I had two stories being enacted – one, of a girl who was studious, serious, prim and proper, and an achiever, uninterested in the 'ordinary' things of life, and another who was soft and vulnerable, interested in dancing, music, and literature, family life – and I even imagined being a popular socialite. I lived and experienced the first story in the external world while the other one largely remained in my private world of fantasies.

I began to do well in academics. I also made attempts to learn dancing and was good at it. I had to give it up against my wishes due to my father's strong disapproval, because he was concerned with the social opinions. Nonetheless, I kept privately listening to music and plays on the radio as much as possible, forcing myself to study the rest of the time, though not always with interest. I managed to pursue violin and singing classes later using a small scholarship awarded to me for good marks in Sanskrit. Music classes provided some diversion from the unhappiness and boredom I felt. My father considered these pursuits an unnecessary distraction which would hamper my academic performance, even though I consistently stood first in my class. I managed to achieve my goal of being a state topper in my eleventh standard in the commerce stream. Journalists interviewed me, and my photograph was in newspapers alongside the examination results. This was like a dream come true, leading to an idea that I could do well in anything with hard work.

Fulfilling the dream of being a state topper left me paradoxically unhappy as it did not lead to any celebration by my family, which I had wished for and expected. It became a burden for me as I was again expected to pursue my higher studies in commerce – a subject I did not enjoy – and maintain the high standard of performance as well. I wanted to study English Literature but, bogged down by elders' advice and expectations, my own confusion and fear of failure (which was instilled in me from various sources as I had not studied in an English-medium school), I chose to study commerce. I rationalised this choice through the fantasy of standing out as exceptional as very few women joined commerce college at that time. College life during graduation was miserable, and my performance dropped from being an academic topper to merely an above-average one.

From this failure-like experience I learnt that I am the one who knows myself and is interested in my well-being – and no one else is. I began to acknowledge the sacrifices and pains in pursuing achievements and realised their meaninglessness if the process of working for them is not enjoyable. I evolved a belief: it does not work for me to make choices based on the pressure of norms and expectations of others or my fears. I can no longer do well in things in which I am not interested.

This belief became significant for the stands that I took about my future studies and profession. I joined a college of my choice for my post-graduation against popular opinions and advice, enjoyed the process, and performed much better. My experience further substantiated my belief and became my ground-rule for myself for future choices, including marriage and potential partners, adding to the possibility of remaining single.

Wishful Thinking and Dreams

In my childhood and adolescence, walking down the streets around my home, I used to look at the houses of people who were married and supposedly settled, and their lives seemed so ordinary and uninteresting. Deep in some corner of my heart was a dream, to be an exemplary woman. Marriage invoked in me the image of a humdrum ordinary life which I did not want.

Nonetheless, while growing up, I did have some dreams about marriage. One part of me wished and hoped for some power to bring a prince charming into my life who would create the extraordinary life of my dreams. However, my attitude and social life (or rather an absence of it), as they evolved over the years, never supported my wishes. I didn't take an interest in relating to boys in college, though some of them tried to befriend me. My family would not have approved of it, and I did not want to provide any cause for disapproval.

Being the youngest of four sisters, I was a witness to the choices my three sisters made or were influenced to make regarding marriage. The lives that they were leading seemed to me mundane, hard, and lacking in freedom. Such a marriage did not seem an attractive option to me. Marriage to me would need to enhance my well-being in life.

When I imagined getting married, I was also unconsciously enacting the prevalent societal assumption that the man be equal or rather better in calibre and financial status. I wished for a well-settled, educated, and brilliant man. But I also wanted someone special – caring and understanding of me as a person. Someone who would marry me for who I am rather than for the dowry my parents would give, the earnings I would bring, or for that matter, the homemaking I would do. Little did I realise that the things I believed made me special were not preparing me to find the kind of man I desired. Hence, whether unconsciously or consciously, I was working to be single as neither I, nor anyone else, was likely to make the efforts needed, given the social norms, expectations, and prevailing practices at that time in the early 1970s.

Disillusionment

I got a job as a lecturer immediately after my post-graduate studies and my family expected me to get married. But my dreams or fantasies about marriage were soon shaken tremendously. To my surprise and dismay, my father, having planted and nurtured in me the dream of being an exemplary high achiever, suddenly turned practical, unambitious, and conservative. When it came to marriage, he was ready to settle for an ordinary man. He assessed my eligibility for marriage by standards entirely different from the qualities I had been encouraged to cultivate. In fact, those qualities had no value in terms of marriage. My parents told me that I was not fair (skin colour) or beautiful, and on top of that, I wore spectacles, and they did not have the money for an attractive dowry. This became the basis for setting aspirations for a life partner for me rather than who I was, what I had become, and what I desired.

My father had a practical plan, endorsed by my elder brothers. It consisted of finding a man who would want me to work as a lecturer. This was a time when men, particularly college lecturers, wanted to marry lady lecturers, assuming that it meant three hours a day of work and lots of vacation to enable them to combine home and work responsibilities most conveniently while earning an equal share of family income. I was disgusted by this thinking. The very thought of such a marriage left me feeling drained. It left me no choice to be either the kind of professional I wanted to be or the kind of homebuilder I wanted to be.

It was evident to me now that my desire to be a professional and be economically independent had matched that of my family, but for different reasons. For my father, perhaps this meant an easier way to find a husband for me, but for me it was a path to professional contribution and a better life. I was repeatedly reminded by my mother of the tiredness and the burdens of my father as reasons to adjust and settle down with whoever was easily available. It seemed that my marriage was not something my parents were looking forward to or had any dreams about. It was for them a duty to be performed for the sake of their image in society.

Though disappointed, due to family pressure, I met some of my father's choices. The marriage proposals presented and the whole process did not feel right for me. I felt undignified hearing conversations on the phone regarding dowry. I resented it and did not want to enter into any marriage in which dowry was a consideration at all, whether less or more. I felt let down, disappointed, upset, and rebellious. I lost whatever trust I had in my family's intentions or capacity to understand or work for my needs, and came to believe that my wishes and future were up to me.

I had deep affection and love for my father, felt a sense of empathy for the enormous responsibility he carried, and was concerned about his health and financial condition. I could imagine then and understand more today where my parents were coming from, given their backgrounds, personal and societal constraints, as well as the disappointment my decisions might have caused them. Nonetheless, I was not willing to accept the choices they made, as for me, they meant accepting a humdrum, dismal future life. I made some efforts through newspaper advertisements, and in fact one possibility that arose seemed promising to me. However, my father dealt with the person with disinterest and disrespect, questioning his suitability on the ground that if I married him, I would need to leave my job and move to a different city. It seemed that based on the experience of the marriage of my eldest sister (who was not employed outside of home), he was unwilling to consider proposals that would mean leaving my job. I imagine he felt burdened with the possibility that if any marriage failed, he would need to support us financially. He wanted the rest of his daughters to have a stable job in order that they would be financially independent in such an eventuality. I was sad and angry at the episode but did not do anything to contact the person and express my views. Instead, I acted from a sense of dignity, social appropriateness, and aloofness, engaging only in wishful thinking that some power would cause miracles – which did not happen. Evidently, I did not have the skills, style, or courage to take charge of the marriage project, so to say.

My Emerging Stand

During this process, I realised that as a woman, it felt riskier to marry someone I did not consider right for me, because it seemed to define my future. For men, marriage was only one part of their life and they perhaps consciously or unconsciously believe that they can shape it the way they want. Therefore, I wanted the person I married to be interested in me as a growing person and open to considering my evolving needs, rather than someone who would define my life's path according to his predefined concepts and requirements. I was not influenced by any readings, theory, or a person. The process as it was happening seemed wrong to my heart and intellect. In a way, I knew quite early the kind of person I would emerge to be, and that I would not be happy in or even endure such a marriage.

Going through this process, despite my fears and doubts, I developed another ground rule for my life: no matter how different, difficult, or lonely the path is, and even at the cost of success in any aspect of life, I must make choices based on my interests and best judgement, because that is what works better for me.

I came to a decision that marriage would not be the primary goal of life. I shall marry only when I believe that I have found the right person and not just because everyone does or because it might be lonely or scary to stay single. I chose to stay with my decision and resist pressures for marriage, both inner and outer, again and again. While I did have concerns and occasionally even fearful dreams about being alone, I was never tempted to change my resolve when I woke up. However, I did not know what it meant to be single or how I would lead a wholesome life as a single woman. I had more clarity on what I did not want than about where I was landing myself.

Finding New Terrains

Coping with pressure from my mother to either get married or leave home, and my dislike for the subject I taught, I developed some unexplainable symptoms of illness. I needed respite from this progressively unbearable situation. I sought and got admission onto a residential doctoral programme at a prestigious institution in a subject of my interest, which enabled me to exit home in what I thought was a dignified and meaningful way, rather than simply staging a walkout. I was also hoping for a better professional future and maybe faintly for the miracle of finding the 'right man' in the new place, with freedom and opportunities. My father disapproved of my decision, pointing to the financial implications and the stability of my current job. I did not get influenced and I was grateful that he did not pressure me to change my decision. My mother was perhaps relieved that I was leaving.

I became a kind of pioneer in my family and the neighbourhood as the first girl to pursue higher education in a prestigious institution away from home. However, when I left, I also carried hurt, sadness, and resentment at my experiences during this phase with my parents. I also embodied in my psyche the ambivalence of society about women's education and work. It defined the course of my life positively in some directions, even as it limited me in other ways.

In my moments of satisfaction with my work and evolving life, I felt a sense of gratitude to my mother for having pushed me to leave, as I had been lingering on in an unbearable situation but doing nothing about my future. I believe it was the grace of universal energy working through her; she became an instrument for change in my life. During my short visits home, I also learnt to appreciate the small things that my father did and healed myself from some of the pain.

I followed my heart and did my doctoral research on 'Lifestyles of District Collectors,' despite the contrary advice from most of my professors that it would be too difficult. I travelled to various districts, made connections with senior government officers, and enjoyed this adventure. It involved an extraordinary amount of work but provided exciting moments in my otherwise-not-so-interesting life. It confirmed my belief that I was unique, that I had a special destiny, and that I need to do what I like rather than follow others' advice or make choices based on convenience.

The Mirage of Marriage

I had read a conversation between W. Somerset Maugham and his woman writer friend in one of his novels.[2] Maugham asked, "Why do nice women marry dull men?" She replied, "Because intelligent

---

2 W. Somerset Maugham, *The Moon and Sixpence* (New York: Washington Square Press, 1968), p. 15.

men won't marry nice women." I have experienced the truth of this statement in my life. My version of it is: "Why don't many bright women marry? Because most men won't marry bright women."

Moving out of the boundaries of home, life in a residential institute brought new experiences into my life. I underwent programmes in personal growth to learn about myself and my relationships. I made new relationships with both women and men. However, my hope or fantasy of getting a proposal from the right man did not come to pass.

After completing my doctoral studies, to fulfil my family's desire and give it one more try, I met some men. The most dramatic meeting was with a doctor whose first condition for marriage was that I continue the college lectureship to earn *and* look after the home. He said he wanted me to provide the financial stability to enable him to lead a relaxed life, as he was very tired (at the age of 31!). The whole episode seemed tragi-comic. It was impossible for me to continue working as a commerce lecturer, which I had disliked even five years before. By then, I had started loving my subject – personal and organisational development – and was looking forward to working in that field. I proposed that we meet a few more times to explore whether there was scope for compatibility, but he wanted a 'yes' – right then. My unwillingness to say 'yes' immediately for him meant 'no.' In retrospect, it seems from a patriarchal man's perspective, I should have been grateful for his willingness to marry me at the age of 30, and should have been desperate enough to say 'yes' immediately.

For the next 15 years or so, I took up new jobs, lived alone in different cities, and learned to shed, step-by-step, some of my self-set restrictions, unrealistic dreams, and relationship patterns. I held good positions and was considered attractive. I experimented with making different and deeper relationships. I wanted to create a circle of friends, both men and women, but even that was not easy. Most women of my age were married, and they often looked at me through the lenses of their judgement, envy, or sympathy, and either kept a distance or withdrew. Nonetheless, I did find a few good women friends, and built friendly relationships with my younger colleagues.

As I stopped relating with a distant, cautious, or 'leave me alone' stance and became more open, the men I met were attracted to me and wanted an intimate relationship. Some of them I shunned from the very beginning. I did make some relationships, hoping each time that it would lead to friendship or turn into a marriage, only to discover that the man's goals were different from mine. The relationships I made lasted only till I realised that reality and withdrew.

Perhaps I had crossed the age for men in our society to consider me marriageable. I imagine that some men saw my being single and attractive as an opportunity for a temporary flirtation, even as they professed intentions of a long-term relationship. I was also learning to be open to receiving care and love when it came my way, which was probably misinterpreted as being 'available.' I sometimes believed the man and began to be drawn into the relationship, partly because it was my nature to trust and I was perhaps vulnerable. For me, however, a commitment was essential to move forward in that relationship. In that sense, the Indian traditional values seemed deep-rooted in me. Hence, the relationship withered away. When I heard the news that the person had gotten married to someone else very soon after that, I was shocked and hurt. It did take time to come to terms with it.

It became evident that I was not seen as a marriageable entity in the eyes of men. I was attractive and special but did not fit into the stereotype of a 'wife.' I was too self-reliant to seem desperate for marriage, and maybe too smart in my work for a man to imagine that I would make his life and career a focus of my life. How right was Amrita Pritam when she said "Indian men are still used to the traditional role given to women; they want intelligent girls for company but not to marry… they have yet to taste and relish the company of mature women."[3]

It also happened with some married men. Why did I get into some relationships with married men? When the person sought me out, he led me to believe that his marriage was meaningless or ending, that

---

3 Amrita Pritam. Retrieved 19 January 2022. Source: https://loveexpands.com/quotes/amrita-pritam-1055551/

I was special, and that he was highly attracted to me. Sometimes, it started with a simple friendship, or an influential man supporting me professionally. I felt good and alive, even if only temporarily. Maybe in my temporary illusion, I did experience a certain amount of happiness, unconsciously imagining that I was truly special because the man was interested despite being married – not knowing how much complexity such a relationship would bring. The fleeting happiness was only followed by pain in the way the relationship evolved. I found that the man's desire to relate lasted only as long as I was not drawn to him, and once I became involved, he tended to withdraw and talk about his marriage and his constraints quite differently. Maybe for the man there was a thrill in achieving the conquest of a competent woman, and I as a person did not matter. I quietly ended the relationship and bore all the emotional consequences without making it difficult for the other person. I was, however, left with self-doubt, as if something might be wrong with me for this to have happened. I also felt hurt and anger, as it seemed an exploitation of my single status. Within me was a deep feeling of being a person who was cherished as special but disowned and abandoned metaphorically. It was the same story as in my family context. Marriage remained a mirage.

Clarity and Acceptance of the Cosmic Plan

I began to realise that to fit into the dominant narrative and possibly not be left alone or lonely, I was ending up finding the wrong men and falling into the trap of dysfunctional relationships. In the absence of a role model and someone whom I could really trust, I was experimenting and learning through a painful process, creating a path where there was no path. I did not want to end up with the regrets of not trying. Later, in my visits to the United States, I came across two books that clarified some of these dynamics.[4] Through my dialogues with some Western women and through my reading, I recognised some of

---

[4] Connell Cowan and Melvyn Kinder, *Smart Women Foolish Choices* (USA: Penguin, 1986); Robin Norwood, *Women Who Love Too Much* (London: Arrow Books, 1986).

my patterns, common amongst many competent women. There was a connection between being an achieving and professionally competent woman and my experience of relationships with men. Also, not having felt cared for or loved in childhood and my growing years, I had a propensity to experience and respond rather disproportionately when men initiated a relationship and portrayed themselves as caring for me.

As I became clear, I resolved that I would no longer be amenable to such relationships. I also realised the meaninglessness of the institution of marriage as it operates today, when so many married men are willing to be untruthful to their spouses. Whether good or bad, it was clear that the belief in fidelity which most wives hold onto seems largely a myth. I evolved the stand that I didn't want to be a wife living in a myth or be a party to the process of breaking up someone's marriage. Thus, my fantasy of marriage as possibly a desirable state ultimately dissolved. I understood the interconnectedness of singlehood with social processes. Some of us choose to be single because of the kind of marriages many others are in and the expectations that marriages impose on both men and women in a patriarchal society.

Sometimes though, it seemed that along with the illusions also went away some parts of me – softness, aliveness, poetry, and some music from my life, which took time to recover in a different, though more enhancing form. My increasing clarity also resulted in a more limited social, personal, and professional circle, leading to more isolation and even impacting my career in subtle ways, as many people find a woman's clarity intimidating.

I have no regrets today. Marriage was something not meant for me, in this society, in this lifetime. I accept this reality. In several ways, I believe it is better than being married. I am willing to relate with men but not in a man–woman relationship. Looking back at my relationships with men, I do not regret them. Instead, I feel grateful that no matter how temporary, socially inappropriate, and heart-rending at the end, they gave me an opportunity to experience what it means to love, to be loved, and to be cherished by a man. I have come to believe that relationships, whether resulting in marriage or not, were not meant to last anyway, in the ways I desired.

Behavioural science work and spiritual practices helped me dissolve any bitterness or regrets. I continue to learn and am perhaps dissolving some of the 'karma' from my past or current life. I realised that I was seeking love, acceptance, care, and companionship outside of myself. Today, I am happy that these relationships ended as they were based on a compromise, unconsciously to fit into the dominant narrative of society, rather than their suitability for me. The wisdom of cosmic consciousness, along with my evolving clarity, ensured that I did not make those compromises and moved forward on a different path.

Professional Life as an Anchor

Simultaneous to the story of these experiences of hope, joy, disappointments, desertions, and an emerging clarity about relationships was my growing commitment to my chosen profession of human and organisational development, which provided an avenue for utilising my experiences, learnings, and the evolving self. My aptitude and ability to understand deeper aspects of self, and to empathise with others and human processes, sharpened over time. I could offer insight into processes at the individual, group, and system level as a facilitator. Maybe this was my way of dealing with pain and predicaments. It enabled me to make meaning out of what I previously felt were strange and often unfair experiences in my personal and professional life. This gave focus, purpose, and meaning to my life.

I also discovered my passion for issues of equity, justice, and freedom for women. I had a propensity to notice, experience, and articulate gender-related processes in any situation, often not noticed or voiced by other people. Over a period of time, with training, I developed expertise in facilitating people to learn how diversity, especially related to gender, impacted individuals and their interactions in interpersonal, group, and organisational settings. However, I focus on empowering people – both men and women – to act with clarity of values for the well-being of all. It is one of my core works in this world in this lifetime, my destiny.

Learning to Value Myself in My Difference

> If there's one thing that moving beyond a fear-based faith taught me, it was that I wanted to be different, or rather, I began to see myself in my full complexity and realized that I was different – and I liked it.
>
> Benjamin L. Corey[5]

While my profession provided a focus and meaning to my life, it was accompanied by some unintended outcomes. I did not seem to fit into the frames people carry of an 'acceptable' woman. Hence, I have often been the target of disapproval, resentment, and envy by them, both in personal and professional settings. As a strong, highly educated, and competent woman who often excelled in what I did, I was perceived as a threat by some and often disapproved of by men in power, resulting in barriers to growth in my corporate job and various difficult experiences in the positions I have held in my professional career. I believe the adverse reactions to my achievements as a single woman have often been unconscious, resulting from sexism and deep-rooted patriarchy. Often even women colluded with men to maintain the status quo of male dominance, despite my speaking up for women's issues.

These experiences left me with bewilderment and pain. The paradox of being single and living alone has been that often, in moments of dilemma and pain, I have had to find support in the very spaces that cause the hurt. Sometimes a residual sense of resentment regarding these processes has left me feeling sad and de-energised. This is a significant facet of being single, especially for those single women

---

5 Benjamin L. Corey, *Unafraid: Moving Beyond Fear-Based Faith.* Retrieved 19 November 2022. Source: https://www.goodreads.com/work/quotes/54491279-unafraid-moving-beyond-fear-based-faith

who live alone. It has been my ongoing inner work to come to terms with this and channel my feelings into learning, creative writing, and other pursuits – converting them into opportunities and emerging emotionally stronger. Currently, my aliveness to my own experiences stays with me not as painful memories or regrets but as a resource in the form of an acute sensitivity to the events and happenings around me. I have learnt to value the difference in me and channel it to bring value to my work as a trainer and consultant, as well as through my writings.

I am clear that I am living my values for myself, without expectation of reciprocity. Deep introspection and spiritual practices supported the process of reaching clarity. As I redefined my expectations in many relationships, understanding, support, and appreciation came from various, sometimes unexpected sources including friends as well as immediate and extended family. I found a few life-long friends amongst my former participants in trainings I facilitated, younger colleagues, and mentees – both men and women.

My willingness to speak my truth, express what I notice, stand up for my values, and focus on group and institutional issues even at the cost of my career (being single probably supported it) resulted in a propensity for me to emerge as a leader and take up leadership roles in institutions, several of them at the Indian Society for Applied Behavioural Science, including serving as its first elected woman president. I also served as the first-ever Indian member elected as the vice-chair of the board of directors at the NTL Institute, USA.

Social Reactions to Singlehood

Why did you choose to remain unmarried? You must be feeling lonely! How do you spend your time? Why don't you stay with your family? Your life is good! You have all the freedom and no responsibility! Why are you busy? What is the work for a single person? Why do you need, or how can you live alone in, such a big apartment (meaning, *anything more than a one bedroom*)? For decades, I have been subjected to questions and statements such as these from relatives, acquaintances, friends, and neighbours. Also, there is sometimes an indirectly conveyed assumption that something is wrong with me, since I did not find a man. Often a response to my personal sharing of any issue is "you should not have remained unmarried" or something to that effect.

These statements and questions used to invoke a host of unpleasant emotions in me. It has taken years for me to come to terms with this and not let it impact my state of mind; and now, I can even laugh them away. I have come to understand that such comments are coming from people's assumptions, fears, envy, sympathy, and other feelings that they project onto me. Such judgemental and presumptuous statements, however, leave little scope for empathy and partnership.

What Do I Feel Good About?

Since I took the courage not to walk the known path but instead to explore the unknown, I have found the profession of life-long interest. I became a pioneer of sorts, and a role model and source of inspiration for many women with whom I came into contact, who long to assert themselves and speak their truth when caught in gender stereotypes and expectations. I have had and continue to have great moments of sharing with my friends, both women and men. Sometimes, I have shared exceptional moments of friendship with men friends, which have been possible only because I was not married to them or anyone else.

I travelled widely as opportunities came my way professionally, without having to get permission from family and without too much guilt. As a corollary benefit, I have been able to play with children in my family across countries. They love to play with me because I am different from their other aunts and grand-aunts. I have experimented with learning new things in my profession and made friends from different countries, which helped me own parts of myself that were not validated in my culture. At a time when the adverse reactions I received as a woman professional in my early thirties in

India had created self-doubts in me, I got support and empathy, as well as validation of myself as a woman and a professional, in my visits abroad. That sense of validation helped me move towards more supportive relationships in India too. I learnt to be feminine in my own unique way and became a stronger person. My relationship with women friends abroad helped me discover new options as a woman in the midst of patriarchy, which is prevalent there as well.

Having succeeded has given me the freedom to fail; having earned has given me the ability to withstand lack of earning; I am responsible only to myself financially, and I do not need to compete or prove myself financially, which frees me to take care of my health and inner well-being. I have the freedom to do nothing and even be in a state of nothingness at times. Today, though I may not be as wealthy as I could be, or as many people are by worldly standards, I feel prosperous.

As a woman, I don't need to prove myself a good wife or mother but I can live to attain inner joy and peace. While I do like to relate to men, particularly if the man is communicative, willing to connect deeply, and is caring, I do not define the meaning and joy in my life through relationships with men, whether their attention, love, or loyalty. Having experienced what love can mean and how temporary it can be, has given me the strength not to get attached to it. However, I do relish the love that comes my way from any source and the experience of it within myself towards others.

What I Missed

There has also been a price to be paid though, and there are things I have missed out on.

There are numerous rituals and celebrations in the family and society that involve marriage and married women, including gifts. There have been rare, if any, celebrations of the significant events of my life because they did not fall into the dominant narrative. The issue is not so much the event or the gifts but the fact that

I never felt the experience of being the focus of my parents' or family's attention or being celebrated in a social context. Further, my sisters brought their life problems connected with marriage, children, or their in-laws to my parents for help. I felt no right to share my problems or ask for help during difficult times in my life since I didn't follow the path chosen by them. Whatever good or bad happened in my life turned out to be my own business. Since I lived away from family to carve out a life for myself, I got excluded from many family occasions as well. My experiences in family as well as work and professional settings have led to a painful realisation that social systems seem to offer greater support to women who have a family. Perhaps because single woman's vulnerability and needs are not seen as important or perhaps there is no witness to watch and judge. Or perhaps because the needs are theirs and not their family's and hence not seen as legitimate.

Apart from the feeling of oddness in social gatherings as a single woman, there is a dilemma even in professional gatherings. Men colleagues gather together while women (mostly their wives), who I don't know, gather together separately. Where do I (a woman who is not a wife and a colleague who is not a man) belong? Do I join the men colleagues' group or the women wives' group? How will it be perceived?

I rarely planned holidays and became a kind of workaholic. My occasional holidays have almost always been combined with work. I also deny myself certain luxuries even though I can afford them, perhaps because, somewhere unconsciously, I wish someone else would organise them for me. Whenever I return home after a long trip, where I have met and interacted with many people, there is a strange as well as deep sense of aloneness and being burdened by having to start my single life again. Finding the groceries, starting my kitchen, serving myself, doing the housekeeping, and so forth – it is different from entering a running home.

Worst Moments as a Catalyst to Spirituality

Vacuum, emptiness, sadness – there have been moments when living alone felt devoid of what seem like the normal things of life, a kind of punishment even in the midst of prosperity, freedom, and independence. It sometimes seemed like I had been left alone as a punishment by society for being capable and competent and daring to walk away from the norm, and both my professional and human potential have been under-utilised. It reminded me of the words of Somerset Maugham: "It goes hard with a woman who fails to adapt herself to the prevalent masculine conception of her."[6] Sometimes, life seems to be a humdrum existence, and I ask myself – is this what I wished and worked for?

There have been phases in my life when I inflicted considerable pain on myself; being unable to take the initiative in relationships, expecting people to reach out to me, an oscillation between high and low self-esteem, and an inability to seek and give love to people who matter. I remember a time in my thirties when I used to experience either pain or complete vacuum and sheer numbness, and between the two, I preferred pain so that at least I felt alive.

At some point during sadness and pain, I had the opportunity to find a spiritual guru – Gurumayi Chidvilasananda. I happened to read a verse from the Bhagavad Gita referred to by my Guru in her writings in which Lord Krishna talks about (as I understood it) "dissolving the union with pain as one of the essential steps in spiritual growth." I recognised my propensity to inflict pain on myself. It was a long and conscious journey to grow as a person who has trust in myself, irrespective of external happenings. My spiritual practices helped me in doing that. Today I feel more blank than pained, more solitude than loneliness, and more quietness than a vacuum.

---

6 W. Somerset Maugham, *A Writer's Notebook* (Great Britain: Penguin Books, 1967), p. 32.

Learning and Growing

I learnt over the years that to be true to myself and live my truth, I need to be willing to let go of anything or everything and anyone and everyone. I have been learning to open my heart to experience the present and trust the grace of the Universe. I learnt to make and experience much out of very little; to build the capacity to live without many things; to enjoy when opportunities arise; give to others without expectations, and say 'no' when I want to. I have realised that it is crucial to take care of my well-being and not sacrifice my health or sanity to be agreeable and acceptable to others. I gave gifts to myself – clothes, jewellery, and whatever things I missed due to being single. I do not hold on to bitterness and have understood that much joy comes in my life albeit differently, outside of socially sanctioned and socially constructed relationships. I experience precious moments with a variety of people and treasure them till they last.

I have also come to understand that my early images or fantasies of a husband were similar to God and depict the eternal spiritual urge to be in communion with God and the highest human self. I had projected that onto a person in my limited awareness: the man I would marry. The essential pursuit is spiritual growth and finding the highest form of love in my own self.

I have learnt that pain also makes me human. And that greed, both for material goods as well as relationships, has no limit – so joy is in knowing when it is greed and when it is need. Relationships are meant to create the capacity in us to experience love, but the source is within. They help make us human but are not permanent in themselves, and one does not need to hang on to relationships as a habit when they are not meaningful. The people in whom you invest may not stand by you, but the Universe creates support from unknown sources too. I have tried to enable myself to manage on my own as far as possible and maintain my physical well-being through a disciplined diet and yoga routine. However, I have found that in exceptional events of dire need, through the grace of the Universe, help comes when asked for, or even without asking. Sometimes a stranger's unconditional help or an unexpected generous gesture has sustained me. I have also learnt to connect more with my family in the last decade.

Perhaps these are things everyone learns or needs to learn, but singlehood pushes you to learn these things for sure sooner and faster – if you want to avoid ending up with greed, bitterness, and regrets, as well as to feel a sense of well-being in your life.

My Dilemmas – Independence, Support, and Connectedness

Dealing with the reality of ageing, illness, and missing out on any given social context to connect with people are the issues I encounter today. As a single woman living alone, there are no taken-for-granted support systems available. I am also aware of my hesitation about asking for support due to dilemmas about dependence – wanting to remain independent, not being a burden, and maintaining my own space. Every time I have to take a conscious initiative, which needs effort to ask for support and accept the consequences of a 'no' or a 'yes.' Part of these dilemmas perhaps are the result of my self-evolved mechanisms and lifestyle to deal with the long years of singlehood.

Living alone, with no regular professional or social forum to connect to, seems to impact my well-being in unconscious and invisible ways – perhaps because it seems very natural and may be essential for human beings to connect socially to live life meaningfully. The very ease with which in a family people argue or take each other for granted, or the mere fact that there are other human beings around, is nourishing in a certain way. I am the one who is always expected to take the initiative to create such settings for myself.

Where Am I Today?

Today, I hold together the feelings of meaningfulness, well-being, and sometimes that something is missing. I feel positively unique sometimes, odd at other times; versatile and innovative sometimes, and overburdened at times. I have had my moments of truth as well as dream-like happenings and experiences, and all of it was enough not to regret.

I am aware that I have somehow sailed through life better than my worst fears, discovering unknown capacities in myself. Life has not always been a cakewalk, but I have chosen to pay the price for living my values rather than regretting failing to do so. It has been meaningful a good part of the time, and I am full of gratitude for this and to all those people who made it happen.

Would I say that I am happy? Not all the time. Would I say I am unhappy? Yes, sometimes. Everything passes, and I shift. I believe that it is not necessary to have happiness (or the absence of pain) all the time. Life is a coexistence of both. To quote the famous Urdu poet Nida Fazli:

> kabhī kisī ko mukammal jahāñ nahīñ miltā
> kahīñ zamīn kahīñ āsmāñ nahīñ miltā
>
> (No one ever gets the entire universe,
> Somewhere the earth and somewhere the sky is missing.)[7]

I mostly lead a calm life and enjoy my own space, independence, and solitude. I do experience joy in togetherness as well. And yet there exists, side by side with this, a longing for an unconditionally supportive, nurturing person in my life – to share life's pains and joys, ups and downs, to be a companion while doing errands, to

---

[7] Nida Fazli. Retrieved 26 November 2022. Source: https://www.rekhta.org/ghazals/kabhii-kisii-ko-mukammal-jahaan-nahiin-miltaa-nida-fazli-ghazals?sort=popularity-desc%20s

consult with when I am in doubt, and who would watch with interest my journey of life. I also know that like a dream, it feels good, but in reality, it is a mirage. I find different people to fill the space and sometimes just experience the void in its uniqueness.

Sometimes, I do wonder whether I have been able to live my highest potential as a human being. I will not leave people behind me – sons or daughters or grandchildren. I have, however, been instrumental in nurturing, intellectually and emotionally, some younger people in their own lives. The process of doing that has given me meaning and joy, and supported them to become competent, responsible, and effective human beings. Yes, often they forget you or even turn against you, but is that not also the story of many parents with their own children? There is also an emerging fear and pain as I grow older that I shall die alone, and none of my family or friends will be there to handle even the last rituals or remember me. At least intellectually, I am also aware that it will not matter when I am no more.

I strive for utilising my full potential and continue contributing to others' lives through what I have learned and am learning. I want to continue to pursue my writing projects and professional work and build a network of people, especially single women around the world, to support each other in pursuing our values and meaning in life. I want to continue investing in my well-being – physical, emotional, and spiritual – and continue to give and receive love and care. I see being single as an opportunity to go deeper into spiritual pursuits and evolve as a human being full of love and bliss before leaving this earth.

*****

Single: Another (Way to Be) Other

Heather Berthoud, USA

Early Experiences as Other

I have a long history of feeling and being other, in some way different from those around me. Born in England of Jamaican parents, I immigrated with my family to the US as a child. The new neighbourhood was mostly Black, unlike our London area that was mostly white. In London, I was British and Black; in the US, I was Black but not American. That difference brought bullying from new classmates and regular disbelief that I did not already know something they all took for granted. I am the eldest of three girls in my family, with a significant age gap between me and the next sister. Growing up with that age difference meant I was made responsible, asked to take care of siblings, understand what they could or would not, and demonstrate a level of maturity and independence I did not always feel. Even within my family, my experiences are not shared, as my sisters do not remember London and had different options and constraints in the US. At the same time, I enjoyed the freedom I was granted – to walk to school on my own, to ride the bus by myself, later to travel back to England as an unaccompanied minor. In a way, I am other in my family too.

Despite such differences, I have had the constant tug of wanting to fit in without losing myself. Whether in the challenge of adopting the American accent so as to ward off immediate ridicule while also wanting to retain what I 'knew' to be 'correct' pronunciation, or learning American popular culture while retaining a love of Jamaican and British foods and habits. I wanted to get good grades and even compete for the top spot without having to be a boy or have my gender questioned, as in, "she's pretty smart for a girl" or "she got even better marks than he did." As a child, my models were women who struck out, stood out, made a mark in the world – Florence Nightingale, Helen Keller, queens, warriors, teachers, Joan of Arc, my grandmother, and my mother. If they were married, that fact seemed secondary to their adventures. Having an adventure and doing something useful seemed more important.

As I got older, my cultural, and sometimes racial, differences created barriers others would not cross. From being teased, ostracised, and ultimately physically bullied in school as a young child for being a foreigner, I found my refuge and success in books and academics. I may not have been like others in the important yet unfathomable ways of assumed culture, but I could get good grades. Unbeknownst to me, this early strategy would reinforce my singleness. I was not pretty, as announced by my glasses, and too smart for boys. As Dorothy Parker said, it was true that "Men seldom make passes at girls who wear glasses," but I did have breasts they wanted to touch anyway. So began the confused and confusing trip into the realm of relationships with boys and men who were inscrutable and treacherous.

An early encounter with boys imprinted on me what I took to be their near-universal disloyalty. As an early teen, I was with a group of friends when one of the boys pulled me aside. After a conversation I have forgotten, he kissed me. My first kiss – ah! Only to overhear him with the group later cashing in on his bet. Small wonder I did not believe they were truthful, kind, or caring of me.

In a family of daughters, my father was the primary model of manliness. His humour, intellectual interests, affection, and sense of responsibility formed my rubric for assessing other men. That he died when I was 13, on the verge of my own emergence, created a disrupted adolescence. Whatever fairy-tale fantasy of happily-ever-after I may have had crashed when he died, even as his example became idealised and therefore unrealisable, in that hazy luminosity that is affectionate memory. Now, my status as the child of a dead parent – not fatherless but not father-present either – combined with my sense of alienation from the culture of the adopted, though not fully owned new home country and mixed in with a sense of not being like other girls enough to warrant whatever good treatment I thought they were getting for being the right kind of girls. I continued to see myself, and be treated, as different.

At about the same time, the US women's movement was asserting ideas of independence, respect, freedom, and exploration on our own terms. Now part of an all-female household, there was no easy fantasy of feminine ease or gendered division of labour for us. Mow the lawn and wash the dishes. Do the laundry and put out the trash. The notion of a man as a sole provider was never the reality even when Dad was alive and impossible with him dead. The idea that my gender should be assumed to attract ease while simultaneously be used as an excuse to prevent me from attaining my fullness seemed especially cruel. All the more so, given that my father had been taken away so that whatever gendered ease might have been imagined was not possible.

I saw around me more examples of strength and independence on the part of women. I witnessed and contributed to my mother's perseverance and our family's resilience. With me cooking dinners, supervising homework, organising myself and my sisters off to school in the mornings, my mother could work and go back to school. I became close to my grandmother, a single woman in Jamaica in the 1940s and '50s, who had her own independence story. I chafed at the expectations that we were a 'broken' family, that without a man, we were incomplete, failing. He had died, not run away. We had been a happy unit until then. Moreover, the presence or absence of a man in and of itself is not what creates wholeness in families. Rather, the presence of love, respect, genuine affection, and a willingness to work together for the individual and collective good constituted our wholeness. The idea of our lack was especially racialised, in that we were fulfilling an American stereotype of a Black-single-woman-head-of-household family rather than discovering and creating our way with dignity and purpose.

The circumstances of my early life created a felt pressure to conform to or disprove stereotypes that had nothing to do with me. In combination with my own disposition, my early circumstances created in me a desire to be fully myself, and to discover what I am capable of without having to withstand the pressure to be someone else for the sake of a relationship or the appearances that others might expect. I did not want to hide my strength. I needed it. I wanted my adventures and to develop my own tastes, to please an audience of one. I understood somehow that life is a creative endeavour, not a script or rule book. The joy is in the creative process.

Singleness Creeps Up

As the creative process of living has unfolded, I see that I am single. My status as a single woman is not chosen in the sense that my occupation is chosen. Rather, it is the accumulation of small and big decisions over the years, informed by a fear of losing what has felt like a nascent self, a desire for an intimacy I have not found, and a commitment to live my adventure in whatever form it takes.

My relationships have been several, some longer than others, but none full enough for me. Whether by my habit or that of the other person, I cannot say, but in no case did I experience a letting go into acceptance of my full person. There was always something the other person wanted me to fix, to do more or differently, to justify or relinquish. When my hopes for being seen and valued finally met the reality of their absence, the relationships ended. I have longed for an abiding companion to my days, a witness to my evolution, a partner in the journey. I have not had one.

I also like my own company. I am happy doing many things on my own – hiking, movies, dinner, writing, reading, painting. So, my daily life is not intentionally solo, but much of it has turned out that way. Along the way, as I do what I like to do, I hope to meet people who share interests and have a mutual interest in each other. That hasn't happened in any way that has led to romance.

As the days stretch into years and decades, I look up and realise that I am single. I don't quite know how to claim it – as status, identity, or something else. It is a status, yes, but also a habit, a groove worn by life events. It is an identity only insofar as it is assigned to me. Not that I reject it. I don't think about it. Yet *identity* has a notion of permanence that *status* does not. Status suggests a condition of the moment, something that may change. Identity seems more of a label, an immutable characteristic that follows the phrase *I am*. Like the way I would say, "I am five foot nine inches" or "I am Black." I don't think of my singleness that way, yet as it is with me longer and longer, it lives with me in much the same way. And has consequences for my life.

I have needed to embrace the (semi?) permanence of singleness as I have planned my life in various stages. As I think and have thought about the jobs to take, the places to live, how to afford health insurance (in the US – worthy of another essay, but I refrain), how to prepare for retirement, possible disability, and long-term care, even how and with whom to vacation, my long-term status as a single woman is central. Once, when visiting a financial counsellor, he asked if I were married or had children. After the customary 'no,' he told me not to bother with life insurance as my death would be a 'financial non-event,' that is, that no one would be concerned about or dependent on my financial remains. And as I have proceeded with the independence necessary to take care of my single self, others assume that I have *wanted* to be alone rather than see a responsible approach to life as I have found it.

In the combination of circumstance, long-term status, and habit, the *identity* of a single woman affixes itself. Yet, it might fall off. I am not committed to it. It is itself a long-term companion to my days, a place of acceptance I return to for as often and as long as I need.

No Language

A college boyfriend I'd not seen in decades recently asked me to summarise my life in a paragraph. I was stunned. How could I describe my life without the easy shorthand that exists for people who are partnered? I could not say, as he did – married, divorced, with a certain number of children. Into those few words, he packed a lot of living. I realised at once that no such language exists as a code for my life. Yet here I am. How can I communicate the richness of the life I've lived without the language that encodes it? Even if people misperceive the particulars of a given experience, the language of coupledom conveys at least a starting point for understanding. No such luck for me.

I am often startled by the surprise that greets my answer to seemingly innocuous questions – "Are you married?" "Do you have children?" – and the dead space in the conversation that follows when I say "no." I am faced with the expectation that my answers should be different. I sense that by not living the script, I am somehow calling it into question. Perhaps because the awkward pause is often filled by an incredulous "why not?" or "what happened?" as though I need to explain my single status. There is no such disbelief or bewilderment when the answer is "yes." I wonder how it would be if the person asking were met with a similarly bewildered "but why?" in response to their "yes." The other typical response is to 'problem-solve' my life with unsolicited advice for how to meet the one (man) I've missed. Often there is simply silence, no query at all. No curiosity about what I *have* done with the time in which I was not doing what they expected. I do not dishonour their life circumstances as easily as they do mine.

There is not a larger cultural sense of what a negative response to the question of "Are you married?" might mean beyond waiting for or scheming towards the possibility of answering in the affirmative.

(I have done that too.) Somehow, I hear in their follow-up questions that my single status says more about me – that I'm unlovable, wrong, too much or too little of something essential, therefore, punished, outside, exiled from the community – than about circumstance. I find the effect intensifies as I have aged past fertility. Or, as my niece said once when she was young enough to parrot social norms without questioning them or keeping discrete silence, "*Weren't you good looking when you were young?*"

I do not have an easy parallel in conversations that centre on spouses or children. There is the assumption that I can't relate or join in. I do not know or engage in things like parent–teacher meetings at school, the search for better summer experiences for the children, what to cook for the finicky eater, how the other forgot to pick up that thing that was most important on the way home. I have separated myself too, as I believed my single status would not be tolerated, included by my partnered friends. Not entirely wrong, but not totally right either. I am not a threat to their relationships. I do not want one of their partners for my own. But I am not available for the couple talk of complaining about the other partner's foibles with knowing glances and exasperated sighs. We can't split off as gendered pairs – women in the kitchen and men watching the TV game. I have a sense – and they have sometimes said – that they don't know what to do with me. Where will they seat me? Who will I talk to?

In India, I was pleased to see that menus everywhere list *veg* and *non-veg* options. There was no mystery about what vegetarians can eat or whether they can be part of the community. In the US, that is changing, but veg. food is often still secondary, available upon request. I see my status as a single person usually like that. In the US several decades ago, the vegetarian option was pasta primavera. It was everywhere and the only option. Now the options are often several and varied. Single status feels like the early days with vegetarianism, when friends were flummoxed and asked outright, "what can we feed you?" "What do you eat?" and restaurants might present steamed vegetables as a meal – no flavour, no protein, no effort or creativity. As though life without meat or partner is inconceivable.

This AND That

I do not have an intimate or romantic relationship, and part of me longs for that, a yearning like a whisper, a faint scent on the wind of my life. Not dominant but there, flavouring the air, seasoning the stew. For a long time, I let the absence of an intimate relationship blind me to other kinds of love – support, connection, seeing, and being seen. The laughter of friends on long walks and in searching conversations.

I do not have to deny my longing nor damn my solitude. I have both. Some days I love my aloneness – the quiet of the house in the morning with me in the sunshine, with tea and my journal. The choice and adventure of carving my own path, of doing what speaks to me now without the need to ask permission or coordinate. And I am missing the reality of accountability to another, of being seen and cherished in intimate ways.

My life has required learning to cultivate happiness. I suppose my partnered sisters have the same need, but I am not deluded by the achievement of a socially sanctioned norm. Recently, I realised, when I was painting for fun, that I had such joy that I talked to strangers, which I thought was so unlike me. But I came to understand that it was unlike me when I'm not full of joy. I had allowed my fear and sense of scarcity to crowd out the natural joy that can be known and experienced as a single woman too. So, one challenge of being single for me is to recall the available abundance, to feel it as deeply as possible, so that it occupies me as joy alongside the fear and scarcity that occupy me as a low anxiety of endless to-do lists and worry about financial security.

Now I am single and not alone. For a long time, I thought they were the same thing, that not being partnered meant travelling the world solo and that single and alone needed to be synonymous. But now I have a household and a friend circle that is more than me. I have a daily connection with people I care about and who care about me. I enjoy sharing meals, ideas, time, discoveries, treats, supplies, errands, laughter, costs, and concerns. I am comforted to know they are here.

So being single is, like life, complex. It is love and loss, joy and grief, in the particular flavour of singlehood. Perhaps not more or less than partnered people, but the same and different too.

Conclusion

I have wanted to feel – and I have not felt, perhaps until now, if yet – that I am fully, enough, securely me to let go into a relationship. I have not met anyone who wanted to join me in such a vulnerable space. So, I have had an enduring status as a single woman. I still do not claim it as an identity, though the strategies for addressing my status have become grooved over time. The status and the strategies needed to deal with it are real, even if they do not fully define me.

*****

Happily Single

Shobha Sarma, India

I am a single woman, a single parent, and have been single for over 30 years. I became single by circumstances, and I have remained single by choice. By nature, I am reserved and prefer to spend time alone by myself. I am happy in my own company, which helped me deal with my single state, but life was not always good.

Childhood – Discriminated Girl Child

I had a sheltered childhood. I mostly grew up in small towns in Kerala, with a few years in Bangalore in between. My parents provided the necessities of life, such as food, clothing, education, shelter, and so forth, but they were not much involved with their children. I realise this now when I look back on my childhood. They did not understand me or my needs – what I needed to make me capable of holding my own in life. I was provided for but not valued. I grew up with an inferiority complex.

I was considered the ugly duckling of the family in my childhood. I was dark-complexioned while my brother and cousins were fair-skinned, and I grew up with the comment, "It's a pity Sabitha's [my mother] girl is dark." It was a painful experience. Added to this was the fact that I was a shy, reserved child – I preferred to be by myself and did not like to be the centre of attraction. I was tongue-tied in most situations and invisible in large gatherings.

As a child, I yearned for parental approval. My mother openly preferred my brother to me – he was an attractive, engaging child. I believe my father had a soft corner for me, but he was not a demonstrative person. The only thing that got me my parents' appreciation was my school grades, where I did better than my brother, and I worked hard not to lose my one advantage.

Yet, when I entered college, I was not allowed to study the subject of my choice. I wanted to study mathematics, but since I would have had to leave home for studies, my parents did not allow that. I had to be satisfied with mathematics as one of my subjects along with physics and chemistry. I hated chemistry, I hated the laboratory with its horrible smells, and somewhere along the three years of the undergraduate course, I lost interest in studies. I graduated with good marks overall, but my grades dropped due to poor performance in chemistry, which lowered my already low self-esteem further. When my parents told me that I could do post-graduation if I wished, I refused. I felt as if I was being set up for failure in some way.

I was artistically inclined from childhood, but again, I did not get much encouragement from my family. My early efforts at creative work were met with wisecracks and laughter. This hurt and made me withdraw more into myself.

When we were children, my brother teased the hell out of me. I was a prey to his pranks all the time. We are very close in age, just 18 months apart. I had the feeling that, since I was the elder one, I had a voice, but his view was that being the male, he had the upper hand. I acutely felt the handicap of being a girl in a patriarchal setup. I felt it most when he followed his vocation and became a chartered accountant with my parents' blessings, while I was not considered important enough to study what I wanted. When he came back from work, my mother would be all over him, offering tea and snacks while I did not even merit a question about how my day went. My relationship with my brother now is what I call 'polite.' We are not close, but with our childhood history together, we are on friendly terms, yet not friends. We live in the same gated community but separate apartments. However, even with a sibling living nearby, I feel I am on my own most of the time.

Since I had refused further studies, the next natural step was marriage. My mother was a homemaker, and I wanted the same. I wanted a nice husband, two or three children, and a comfortable home. I wanted to be the queen of my house. I had no ambitions for a career dealing with files, clients, or the telephone. Somewhere in my subconscious mind, I wanted a perfect family, which would make up for my ugly duckling years. Looking back, I can see how naïve and foolish I was.

I would never 'meet a boy and fall in love,' and arranged marriage was the way to go with my kind of family situation. When the proposal came, it seemed good enough for me. I gave my consent. I never thought of anything going wrong. 'Wrong things' happened to others, in books and newspapers, not to 'us'; now I realise how stupid I was.

Marriage and Divorce

I was married at the age of 21, and my marriage lasted just over four years. It was an abusive relationship, physically, mentally, and emotionally. I was a punching bag for my husband, who turned out to be addicted to alcoholic drinks. The first year was not so bad, but things took a turn for the worse after my daughter was born. I felt that he was expecting me to be a teddy bear in between the punching sessions, which confused and terrified me more. I was naïve and innocent, so much so that when my husband got drunk the first time, I did not even realise that he was drunk. I was shocked out of my senses by his behaviour. I gave birth to my daughter around 15 months after my wedding. The physical violence started after this, and soon our relationship reached a point of no return. It was a joint family, but not one person in the family came forward to help me. I withdrew more and more into myself.

I did do my best to make the marriage work. I tried to talk to my husband, his family, and his friends. I suggested Alcoholics Anonymous. I even met with a doctor to know if any drug might make him give up drinking. Soon I realised that it was hopeless; whatever I tried would work only if the person I was trying to help admitted that there was a problem and wanted to be supported. Neither he nor his family acknowledged that his behaviour was not normal. According to them, I had to put up with whatever he did to me because it was his right as my husband. I somehow survived through three years of this hell. The fact that I had a child to care for kept me going. My hobbies also helped; my craft and needlework kept me sane during those turbulent years. In desperation, I once attempted suicide, which made me realise that continuing in this situation would either drive me insane or leave me dead. I had a responsibility towards my daughter; she deserved a better life. So, a few days after my daughter's third birthday, I walked out of my marriage, never to return.

Being from a small community, the Gowd Saraswat Brahmins, my rebellion created a lot of noise, and I earned some notoriety for my decision to dump my husband. Some of the extended family cold-shouldered me. There were judgements, preaching, and even sniggers. People who misunderstood my reserved nature for arrogance rejoiced, thinking that I had come by my just deserts. If my husband had dumped me, perhaps I would have been vilified but also earned some sympathy. If I had been widowed, I would have probably got sympathy but would be an outcast at family gatherings. The fact that I filed for a divorce and dragged the matter to court was unforgivable. How dare a woman say 'to hell with you' to her husband!? But I had had enough. I decided to go ahead and face it head-on. And I succeeded after a bitterly contested divorce. I also won custody of my child.

A Phase of Loss and Failure

The divorce closed one chapter in my life but opened the next round of chaos and confusion. My parents brought me back from my marital home and, to do them justice, I must say they did a lot to rehabilitate me. I was on the brink of a nervous breakdown, and it took me a few months to recoup. My family was not very well off, and I needed to earn to provide for my daughter. My father got me a job, and my mother stepped in to look after my daughter when I was away at work. They gave me support, but it came at a price. While I did not starve and had a roof over my head, I did not have peace of mind. It was their household, I was a dependent, and I had to conform to their way of doing things. I had indeed lived with them for 21 years before my marriage, but I was not the same naïve, innocent girl now; I was a woman, a mother, and I had grown up during those four years of marriage. They often forgot I was an adult. I needed help but not to be under someone's thumb. Their idea of hand-holding was to tell me exactly what to say and do in a situation and, in the same breath, tell me that I had to be independent. They did not consult me when they made any major decision. They found fault with my parenting style; I could not even decide for my daughter at times. I was also not allowed to forget their magnanimity – many times, I heard the words, "your coming back to us has spoiled the quality of our life." I acknowledged this truth but resented that it was shoved down my throat so often.

With the divorce, I lost a chunk of my early life. My ex-husband and his family probably felt rejected and humiliated by me, as I had asked for divorce. So, when I collected my belongings from my ex-husband's home after the divorce, they did not return some items, precious to me but of no value for them – my album with school and college photographs, my craft books and tools, my daughter's storybooks and toys. When I inquired about them – they denied finding them in my room. Coupled with post-traumatic stress, this created gaps in my memories. I do not remember certain people or events. I have forgotten all but one or two of my schoolmates and many of my college contemporaries. With no photographs or memorabilia, my mind was blank about many events, which somehow enhanced my feeling of being alone in life. Pleasant memories of friendships and events in school and college were lost, and I was left with the bad memories of my failed marriage.

I had a lot of anger and bitterness festering inside me, but there was no way to vent these feelings. There was no one to listen to me without judging me. I bottled up most of my feelings inside me, and when sometimes the pressure was too much, my daughter bore the brunt of my outbursts. I feel sorry for that, but I don't think I would behave any differently if I had to live my life all over again in the same circumstances. As a result, my daughter and I had a love–hate relationship for many years.

The divorce made me feel I had somehow failed as a wife. My ex-husband died nearly a decade after the divorce (alcohol killed him in the end). Though I had opted for the divorce to preserve my life and sanity, there was always a doubt in my mind – had I done the right thing or was there anything else I could have done to save the marriage? When I heard of his death, I knew that I had walked out at the right time, when I was still young enough to start my life over again. If I had stayed in the marriage, I would have been ten years older and probably a mentally disturbed woman, unable to make a fresh start in life. I can't even imagine how my daughter would have turned out living in that violent atmosphere.

Also, life as a single parent was not easy. To be both father and mother to my daughter was doing double duty and very tiring. I needed to earn my living but also be there for her when she needed me. There was no one to share the responsibilities and bounce ideas off regarding the best for my child. Criticism of my parenting style by my parents made me feel that I was a failure as a mother as well. But my tussles with my daughter reduced a bit as she grew up. I also changed jobs, and my new job was something I enjoyed. I did not have to answer telephones or deal with irritable customers. Life got a bit better, and I felt maybe I was not such a failure after all.

Then fate intervened again. When my daughter was doing her undergraduate studies, my father decided out of the blue that they did not want to live with me anymore. My mother said she was tired of housekeeping. Her complaints increased day by day, and none of the solutions I offered, including a full-time maid, found favour with them. I could not quit my job to stay at home for them. My daughter had not completed her education, and till she got settled, I could not give up working. My parents decided unilaterally to move in with my brother, without discussing it with him or me. So, we separated – I moved to a small flat with my daughter and my parents with my brother, who had his own family by this time. My mother had never given up her position as the lady of the house to me, and I did not understand why she would want to give it up to her daughter-in-law. I felt that somehow I had failed as a daughter as well.

However, even after we separated, my parents were unwilling to give up control. I had been under their thumb for so long that, initially, I found it difficult to assert myself. A few years passed before I shook off the shackles of parental control.

Healing from the Past

Living on our own threw up a lot of challenges, which created new problems with my daughter. She completed her post-graduation and started her first job. When she moved to her second job, she became financially independent. She refused to participate in any way in the running of the house and was always out with her friends, coming home late and altogether rebellious. She wanted to move out, and finally, tired of the constant fights, I let her go. She moved into a paying guest accommodation near her office and came home only on weekends. But this state of affairs did not last long. Four months was all it took for her to realise the importance of home, and she was back. That was the turning point in our relationship. We gradually became friends, and now she is incredibly supportive of me.

Even my parents have come around. After being in charge for 40 years, they found that living as dependents was a different ball game, and they took time to accept it. They finally admitted that they had been rather unfair to me. And I received my share of parental appreciation, which I had missed in childhood.

My sense of failure as a mother and daughter no longer haunts me. As to my feeling of failure as a wife, I realised that I did not have to be a 'wife' to be a success. From this moment, I started loving myself.

While my ex-husband's death released me from self-doubts, what led to my healing was my decision to forgive him. A year after I moved out to my own flat, I read the story of a woman who forgave her son's murderer and how it helped her to come out of her trauma. I understood that I needed to forgive the people who had hurt me, to move on and be happy. Holding grudges was making me miserable, not them. I needed to forgive for my own sake, not because they deserved it. I made a ritual out of it. I went to the temple and asked God for strength to forgive all those who had hurt me in my life, including my ex-husband, his family, and also my family. I also forgave myself for the blunders I had made in my anger and frustration. I felt so light and clean after I let go of my anger and resentment. I have not forgotten, but I have learned not to remember. When I let go of negative thoughts, it made space for positive ones to enter my mind. I have progressed a lot on my spiritual journey after forgiving all those who hurt me in the past. Forgiveness also resulted in the restoration of my faith in the Almighty, which I had lost for some time. I learned the power of prayer. Since then, with conscious practice, I have achieved what I call detached attachment to a great extent. I care, and I empathise, but I am not overcome by emotions anymore. The only person who can still push my buttons is my daughter, but this is also getting less and less frequent.

Freedom to Be, Learn, and Have Fun

At the age of 48, I felt it was time for me to take a break. I had held three jobs in 22 years with an interval of two years in between. I had enjoyed my last job in the medical transcription field, and it gave me the confidence and financial stability I needed. During the 20 years of working life, I had saved enough to live a reasonably comfortable life. My father had instilled the saving habit in me, and I had lived a simple life with no luxuries for over two decades. I bought only essentials, rarely took vacations, did not party or entertain. I walked to save bus fare. I was firm with my daughter when she demanded things I could not afford (this was another reason for our love–hate relationship). I took tailoring orders for a while and worked late into the night after returning from work to earn a little extra money.

After working for nearly 11 years in my last job, I felt saturated. Working at a computer for ten hours a day was extraordinarily fatiguing, and I started to develop health problems. Working long hours on the computer created eyestrain and wrist and shoulder pain. I had had to drastically reduce my needlework and crafts to save my eyes and hands. I was also diagnosed with fibromyalgia, albeit a mild case. I wanted to enjoy life and the money I had saved when I still had the health and energy. I felt that if I continued working until I was 58, which was the retirement age, I would end up paying my life savings into the doctor's pocket.

I wanted to rest and relax. I wanted to get back to my hobbies. I wanted to have coffee while leisurely reading the newspaper in the mornings. I wished to sleep in, read books, listen to music, watch TV, and generally take things easy. I reworked my finances, closed my housing loan, and then quit my job. Soon after this, my daughter married and left home. I was alone now, and a new chapter opened in my life.

I was truly free at the age of 50. I rediscovered my hobbies – embroidery, dress-making, crochet, doll making, amongst others. I attended workshops to learn new forms of art like the Ojo Di Dios and mandala drawing. I had always wanted to learn Sanskrit, and I took an online course. I took classes at home for some of my crafts. I recently took part in an exhibition and sold some of my creations. I had dreamt of travelling but never had the money or the time for it. I started going on tours with a travel group for women and then later with a travel company for people above the age of 50. I surprised myself by finding that I was comfortable travelling with strangers, including sharing a room with someone I had first met just a few hours before. I have had more fun since turning 50 than I ever had in the 50 years before it.

Single Women Across the Globe Workshop

My daughter sponsored me for the 'Single Women Across the Globe workshop' held in Jaipur in November 2018. I was a little hesitant since I felt it might rake up unpleasant memories. I thought I had healed from my traumatic past, and I did not want to look back. My daughter was insistent; she told me that this was the litmus test, that I would know whether I had truly healed, and if not, whatever cobwebs left would be swept away. Finally, I agreed to go, and I am glad I did.

The workshop was a revelation. Listening to other single women sharing their experiences, I realised how far I had come in my journey. I had progressed much further than I had thought I had. Meeting a sisterhood of single women, I was able to connect with the similarities and appreciate the differences in our life experiences and our responses and coping mechanisms. I was amazed at the ease with which we opened out to each other. I surprised myself by sharing thoughts that I had never shared with anyone, whether family or friends. At the end of the workshop, I felt a deep sense of gratitude for the blessings in my life.

As a part of the workshop, we met with some single women being trained to be drivers for cabs for women. I listened to a woman whose experience of marriage had been similar to mine. She was abused and beaten up by her husband, and she left him. She said that it took her just two years to recover and get back to normal. I wondered how this had been possible. She had had no support from her parents or siblings, yet she had managed to get back on her feet in two years while I, who had had some amount of support, had taken 20 years to heal. Discussing this during our sessions, I realised that for me, marriage had meant much more than just security. I had looked forward to love, companionship, romance, family, home, and I was ready to do my share of work along with my husband towards achieving these goals. The fact that he did not share my sentiments, that I was just someone to punch or hug as his emotions dictated, broke me. It was a total disillusionment, and it took me two decades to heal from my wounds and realise my sense of self-worth.

Discovering Myself

As I mentioned before, I became single due to circumstances but remained single by choice. I was so traumatised in my marriage that it took me years to interact naturally with men. I had proposals for a second marriage, but I refused. I had no intention of getting trapped again. The very thought of being alone with a man in the bedroom scared the daylights out of me. I had experienced real terror in my married life; I was reduced to a shivering, cringing wreck on many nights. I was not going to allow a man to have that power over me again. But over the past few years, I have noticed a change in my outlook. I am not scared anymore. I have developed friendships with a few good men, platonic in nature. I realise that not all men are monsters. I am not actively looking for a relationship, but the Universe has given me many unexpected gifts, though late in life; who knows what else is in store for me? My life has always progressed in a reverse manner. I wore sarees during my college years and later moved to salwars,[1] skirts, pants, and dresses. I slogged in my youth scrimping and saving and worrying, but I am having fun in my fifties. I am not an ugly duckling anymore, though I may not have become a swan. So I now keep my options open.

During the workshop, some of the participants expressed that they had physical needs, and it was one of the challenging things about being single. It felt strange that I had never felt that in my life. I have been celibate for over 30 years. I did not miss the physical part of

---

[1] The sari was traditionally an Indian dress for adult women while skirts, pants, and dresses were for girls.

a relationship; what I missed was the emotional part. On thinking back to my married years, I realise that I did not care for physical intimacy. In an arranged marriage, one falls in love after getting married, and I never got to the point where I fell in love with my husband. Maybe that is why I was not comfortable. My marriage had lasted just four years, out of which three were traumatic, and I assumed this made me 'cold' towards men. It certainly was part of it, but now I think it is more deep-rooted. Another curious observation was that many women expressed that being single made them vulnerable in their work places and easy targets for sexual harassment. That was something I had never faced in my career. Of course, there were the usual experiences in crowded buses and stares and comments in public places, but no one ever propositioned me at my work place. My female colleagues told me that I was called the Ice Queen by the men behind my back. I wonder what kind of vibes I gave out to be labelled this way. The interactions in the workshop set me thinking, and I now strongly suspect I am asexual or what is informally called an 'Ace.' Since then, I have read up on this, and I am discovering unexpected facts about myself.

Yet I have always been a romantic at heart, and despite all that happened in my life, I still remain a hopeless, incurable one. I read romantic novels and sigh, listening to romantic songs gives me goosebumps, and I watch romantic movies and shed tears. I have also had my share of crushes but have never carried any of them forward. I prefer romantic daydreams – which are safe, as they can always be manipulated to have happy endings. Perhaps I am a demi-sexual, but I guess I shall never know for sure. I am still exploring this aspect of my personality.

Lessons Learnt in Life

Having struggled to make ends meet, I have learned that money may not buy happiness, but lack of it can cause a lot of unhappiness; you need to have enough to grease the wheels of life. I learned the hard way that every woman needs to be financially literate and independent, whether married or single. I encouraged my daughter to study what she wanted and made sure she took up a career of her choice. I did not want her to repeat my mistakes and suffer in life.

I have learned that I should not depend on anyone for my happiness; I have to make it myself. I realised that happiness could be the journey, not just the destination. I have learned to love myself. I have learned to self-validate and not look to anyone for validation. I have learned to reward myself and not wait for others to appreciate me. And in the workshop, I realised that I need to communicate better, to say what I feel and think and not keep it inside me. I also learned that I communicate better through writing than speaking.

When you love someone, love enough to let go – this is another lesson in my life. If they belong to you, they will come back; if not, they were never yours. I let my daughter go when she wanted her freedom, and she returned to me. I accepted my parents' decision to leave me though I felt hurt and rejected; I later gained their respect. Let go, live, and let live – this is my mantra now.

I also learned that gratitude is the way to contentment. Despite all the troubles I have had, I have a lot to be grateful for. I am grateful I had the strength to walk out of an abusive marriage before it was too late. I am thankful that my parents took me in when my marriage fell apart and helped me rebuild my life despite their life getting messed up. I am grateful that I have a loving, supportive daughter who understands me. I am thankful for my friends, who are more like family. I am grateful that I was successful in my struggles to make something good out of the mess in my life. And finally, I am grateful that I have so many things to be grateful for.

Living Life on My Own Terms

Being single has its merits. I am free to do what I want with my life and my time. If I feel like spending the day in bed reading, I do it. If I feel like binge-watching TV, I do it. As I am not a lazy person by nature, such days are few and far between, but it is nice to know that I have the freedom of choice. I dress to please myself. I cook the dishes I like, and I don't need to cook every day. I got my wish to be the queen of my home, albeit in a different sense. I keep myself busy with my creative hobbies, which give me a lot of joy. I pack my bags and head out on a tour without having to worry about home and family. Recently, I went to watch a movie alone in the theatre, and I enjoyed the experience. I find being single very liberating. I enjoy the solitude and the sense of freedom that comes with being single.

The only time my single state bothers me a little is when I am sick. But the wish that there was someone to take care of me is tempered by the thought that if I was not alone, I might have had to look after others even when I am sick (that is the fate of most women I know). As it is, I can just go to bed and not bother about anything. Yes, there are times when I feel the need for someone to talk to, someone to laugh with, someone to sit with in comfortable silence but, by and large, I am content being single. I know myself, and I am my own best company.

I was largely misunderstood as proud or arrogant because of my reserved nature. I am not antisocial, just differently social. Now I am not as shy and reserved as I was many years ago, but I still need solitude and time alone. I do not like crowds and loud, noisy parties. I prefer small gatherings and one-on-one interactions. But I am comfortable meeting new people and travelling with strangers. I have made many good friends through my travels. I have also made lasting friendships in my workplace, and we are in touch even after I quit my job.

I may not be a talker, but I am a good listener. My friends confide their problems to me, and whether I give advice or not, they feel better for having talked to me because I listen to them. I have been an agony aunt to many people. Listening to other people's problems has taught me to be grateful for my blessings. Having achieved a certain degree of detachment, I can empathise without getting unduly affected and emotional. I have a small circle of close friends who I know would step in if and when I needed help.

Among my friends, I never found any difference in attitude because I was a divorcee. Over the years, I have received appreciation for having had the courage to walk out of an abusive relationship. Those relatives who sneered earlier are now mostly silent. When I retired early, people were envious. There are those odd relatives who pass double-edged remarks in my hearing, but I have learned to ignore them – they are not worth stressing over.

As I look at the future, I can see it will not be easy to be single and ageing. I realise that I would need help, at least with the instrumental activities of daily living like cooking, shopping, and house-keeping. My daughter wants me to live with her, but I do not wish to do that. She and her husband are busy with their lives. We are on excellent terms now, and I do not want to upset the equation. I have made up my mind to move into a senior living community when the time comes. I would be cared for, yet I would be independent. I want to do this when I am still able to select the place myself; I don't want anyone else to decide for me. I am slowly but surely approaching the stage where (to quote one of the dear ladies in the workshop) I can change the light bulb, but I need someone to hold the ladder, and I am preparing myself for it.

I have just two regrets: one, that I never had a romance in my life that swept me off my feet (never mind how it ends!); and the other, that I never learned to ride a bicycle. I do not regret anything else; all that happened, happened for the best. It made me what I am today. For a long time, I did not love myself, I did not consider myself lovable, but now, as Kareena, the heroine of *Jab We Met* (a Hindi movie, whose title means "when we met") says, "I am my own favourite person."

On International Women's Day, many syrupy messages go around about women being loving moms, caring sisters, understanding wives, and lovable daughters. I do not identify with any of these labels. I just identify myself as a woman, a human being. If I had to use adjectives, I would say strong, reliable, empathetic, independent, loyal, and creative. I am also utterly feminine, and I love being feminine. If I had to take birth again, I would want to be born a woman in my next life.

I have healed from my past. A few scars remain; they may itch at times, but they will not get infected again. The scars prove that I have lived, not just existed. The Universe has responded positively to my efforts at taking charge of my life, and maybe in the future it will arrange for cosmetic surgery of my scars as well.

*****

Why I Chose to Remain Single: To Get Freedom *from*, Freedom to, or *Inner* Freedom?

S. Uma Devi, India

The Shaping of My Values and Aspirations

Born as the eldest child in a South Indian family that had migrated to Delhi, I had to cope with two cultures – one at home and another outside home. Like any other first-generation migrants, who generally like to maintain their culture at home, my parents tried to keep up their South Indian culture at home – food, customs, rituals, language, music, and so forth. However, they also encouraged us to mix with children of families belonging to the local area or those belonging to other parts of India. Thus, to some extent, we were cosmopolitan. The other institution which had a significant influence on me was the Sri Ramakrishna Mission, as my father was an ardent devotee there. Hence, we moved closely with the *sanyasis* (Hindu monks) of the Ramakrishna Mission. They visited us as we occasionally invited them to have food at our place. We had seen that the *sanyasis* who were not married and did not have a family were respected very much. I thought of becoming a *sanyasini* (a

Hindu nun) very early in life, to lead a spiritual life. We often heard highly of Ramana Maharshi, a realised Soul and whom my father had the opportunity of meeting. The lives of Sri Ramakrishna and 'Sri Sarada Ma' (the Holy Mother) were set up as role models. As we understood, the goal of life was to lead a spiritual life to realise one's real self. We heard lectures from very well-known *sanyasis* (male monks) such as H.H. Swami Ranganathanandaji on Srimad Bhagavad Gita, Upanishads, and the other Hindu scriptural texts.

Our parents placed a lot of importance on our education, yet when I was 17, my father started talking about my marriage. However, my mother insisted that I should at least be a graduate and should be able to stand on my own feet if required. She had her elder sister's experience in mind, who was widowed at the age of 21 and had two small children to bring up. She undertook further studies after she lost her husband, to become a school teacher and raise her children. This incident had changed the outlook of my mother and her other sisters about women's education. However, they were not so much in favour of women becoming too professional. According to them, only in time of need should women be able to supplement the family income.

So I could complete a B.A. Hons. (graduate degree) in economics but, after that, my mother was not in favour of my doing an M.A. (post-graduate degree). Instead, she thought it would be better for me to do a B.Ed. (bachelor's degree in education) for the reason that I would be older if I did an M.A. (a two-year programme, whereas the B.Ed. was one year), and therefore I would be over-age for marriage. Moreover, a school teacher's job would not interfere with my family life, but if I took up a more professional career, I wouldn't have enough time for the family.

After obtaining the B.Ed. degree, I became more interested in my subject and wanted to do a master's (M.A.). My mother resisted, and now my dream and her dream clashed. Being the eldest in the family, she wanted to get me married off. Even though I had said that my other siblings could be married off, she was not agreeable to this as she said people would think I have some physical disability. Hence, if one did not get married, many people would assume that the person has some disability or has been jilted in love and so on.

Moreover, for her, the very thought that I would remain single was not acceptable. She was also scared that I might become a *sanyasini*. Here I found some contradiction in my parents' thinking. On the one hand, we grew up thinking that they held *sanyasi*s in high regard, but when I came to choosing that way of life, they were not happy.

Standing up in Pursuit of My Ideals and Goals

I rebelled and, after teaching in a school for two years, joined an M.A. in economics. I understood that freedom is taken and not given. However, I must clarify that I was seeking freedom *to* and not merely freedom *from*. I was not escaping *from* something but was very clear about my life's goal; and thus, for freedom *to* pursue my passion, I had to be free *from* certain other things. In this context, I must also mention that I was now part of a discussion group that had come up around Dr. S.N. Mukhopadhyaya, a professor of education and social sciences. He was a social philosopher and a visionary. Two of my colleagues in the college where I was teaching in Delhi used to be part of this discussion group – a philosophy teacher Dr. Mrs. Teresa Vijayan, and a commerce teacher, Uma Jain, who is the editor of, and a contributor to, this book. We have shared precious moments in the early part of our professional life, and writing this article brings nostalgic memories of those times, as well as being a meaningful reflective exercise on these issues after 45 years of our singlehood.

In this group, we discussed anything under the sun. The main topics of discussion centred around questions we were facing in our personal lives in the context of the then social reality, including marriage and singlehood. We tried to imagine as social scientists what kind of society would be ideal – utopia. Our discussions reminded me of the Socratic method or the Upanishadic method, where the teacher and taught discussed threadbare every aspect of life philosophically. It was not merely a theoretical quest but was very real – a realistic quest where we got answers to what one should do. It was not merely pragmatic either. We understood how much British colonial rule in India has colonised us and how our indigenous systems of knowledge and social mores were jeopardised by the Western notions of democracy and secularism, through the superimposition of the British parliamentary system, the American presidential system, and the Roman judiciary. These were alien to our culture. Moreover, economic planning started as a technical exercise, which did not consider these cultural factors. I am mentioning all this because these made me an activist as a social scientist in my own way. I started by thinking of my own life. I realised that migration was part of that process of colonisation, and I became conscious of what it had done to my family and me. As a result, I was keen to go back to my roots.

The goal of my life was becoming clear to me. The purpose of life for me was *moksha*, which is liberation and self-realisation. At that time, I had only a vague idea of all this, but it was a powerful thought, and I wanted to work towards it. I had come to understand that marriage would stand in the way of my pursuing this goal, so I resisted it. My mother could not understand this, nor could my extended family members (aunts, uncles, and cousins). Although I opted out of marriage, as a single woman, I nonetheless had my own way of relating to society, my immediate family, the extended family, the workplace, my profession, and to my goal of leading a spiritual life. The challenge was to blend the individual and the social.

A major decision that I had to take was about reverse migration to South India, to the place from where my parents had migrated. This decision was well thought out and discussed with my like-minded friends. I had a permanent job in a college in Delhi as a lecturer. Now I got a higher position as a reader at a university in South India where I could also pursue my Ph.D., which was about the economy of the region to which I migrated.

Having decided to take up this job, I had to arrange for my accommodation. I had not lived outside my home till then. Moreover, I was conscious that I would need physical security. I chose to remain in an *ashram* with a hostel for women run by *sanyasinis* of the Ramakrishna Sarada order. The then president of the ashram was Revered Pravrajika Ajayaprana Mataji (sanyasinis of Sarada Mission are addressed this way), who gave me all the support I needed then. She was and is a source of inspiration to me. Staying in the ashram hostel gave me an identity and the security I needed in a town not known to me. I was also conscious that some men in my workplace would be wondering what kind of person I was – a single woman coming from Delhi. Unlike people in Delhi, who knew my family and my antecedents, no one in my new place of work knew me well.

Interestingly, the town I came to settle in has a temple for a goddess who is unmarried. It is near Kanyakumari, where also the goddess is unmarried. In Hindu mythology, the unmarried woman 'a *Kanya*' is worshipped! These religious symbols at that time inspired me further.

Repercussions of My Decision on My Family

My mother could not accept this decision of mine to stay alone in a different place. She took it to her heart and suffered a stroke after a year of my leaving Delhi. There was pressure from the family to return to my old job in Delhi, where I had a lien. However, I resisted this. It was a very challenging situation emotionally, to cope with the bitterness in my familial relationships. Also, my mother needed care and to be looked after. The challenge was to help in taking care of my mother and yet to continue my pursuit. My mother and others in the family were not agreeable to the idea of moving her to the place where I was working. Yet, I applied for a staff residence at the university. They were called 'family quarters,' so its allotment to a single woman was objected to by some persons.

The professors' quarters were large and of the bungalow type. However, since I said that I would be bringing my parents, they allotted one to me. I engaged a lady cook and housekeeper to help me run the household. My family members, along with my parents, came from Delhi every year during the winter season and spent two-to-three months with me. Since I was staying within the campus, it was easier for me to attend to my work and family. Moreover, there was a full-time person to help with household chores. However, I was sorry that I could not do more than this for my mother, when she had made so many sacrifices to rear us. A large part of the burden of taking care of my mother fell on my younger sisters and brother, who were also in academia like me. Being the eldest sister, I had a motherly relationship with my siblings. Mother lived for six years after her stroke. She could participate and do certain things despite having become dependent due to some physical disabilities. This was the period when I was also doing my Ph.D. Just a week before my mother's death, my viva-voce was over. In fact, before her death, she asked me how I had performed in the viva-voce and was happy to know that I had fared well.

After her death, the responsibility of arranging my brother's and sister's marriages fell on me, and I took it up. Since we were brought up in a tradition where arranged marriage was the norm, my siblings also did not find their marriage partners. So, I decided to help my father find suitable partners for them and arrange their weddings. Father was alive when my brother got married, but one sister got married after his death. The other sister opted to remain unmarried. During this period of emotional turmoil, I must say my friends both in the ashram (who were also single) and from my earlier discussion group in Delhi were very supportive. I had friends to whom I could open my heart and share my agonies. They always stood by me. It is a great blessing to have good and trustworthy friends. This is true for all but perhaps more so for a single woman.

Living as a Single Woman in the University Quarters

I was not the only single woman living in the staff quarters. There were some others but very few. It was interesting to see how the other professors and their wives viewed me. Some were curious and even nosey, watching out to see who was visiting me. Some others were very protective. However, if I came home late in the evening, most of them who would meet me on the way would enquire why I got so delayed. It was not very safe for women to come back alone at dusk and late in the evening, as some drunken people were moving around at that time. So, there was a genuine concern as well as curiosity. My male colleagues would generally not visit me at home, which suited me. Many took my cook to be my mother. It seemed to add to my respectability, as I was not living alone. Since I did not like to keep a TV, some women would pity me, saying being single, "don't you feel lonely?"

Gradually people got to know me. My uncle and aunt started coming and staying with me during part of the year, and the other family members – parents and siblings – also spent a few months with me during the year. I lived for nine years in the quarters but eventually decided to build my own house.

As a Single Woman in Professional Spaces

As a single woman in the workplace and professional organisations, I had to keep a stiff exterior so that men did not make advances. I found that many men were not used to women interacting professionally with them on an equal footing. In the department staff council, some of my colleagues took my general comments on some issues very personally and became defensive. One or two would make comments to others on my body language, behind my back, although not in front of me. The male administrative staff did not like to take orders from a woman. Some of the male students also were not very comfortable in my presence, particularly when they did not know something. Not many males visited me in the quarters. However, many years later, some male research students visited me and had long discussions with me at home.

I had become very active in the professional association in economics. Women in the professional association felt that they should also have a role in the executive committee and so voted for me. I came to occupy positions in the executive committee. Some men felt uncomfortable associating on equal terms with women, while others would be very helpful and make space for women. However, generally, I had found that men with traditional values were very respectful, but others in the name of modernity tried to take advantage of women.

Relationships as a Single Woman House-Owner

I decided to build a house for a few reasons. One was that I found that the university authorities were continually trying to make me realise that they had done me a favour by allotting me a bungalow. Eventually, they started suggesting that I become the warden of the women's hostel, offering free quarters as a perk. I was unwilling to become a warden as that would give me less time for my academic pursuits. Secondly, I had offered to take care of a lady leading a saintly life – H.H. Santa Devi. Here I must mention that after my mother's death, I felt somewhat guilty that I could not take care of her. The idea of taking care of someone who is not my blood relation often came to my mind to get over this sense of guilt. When I came to my native place, I met H.H. Santa Devi, who was known to my father and his family. She was also my father's sister's classmate and later had become her spiritual mentor. I found her and her lady disciple, who was taking care of her, to be unique. They were educated and very liberated, yet not in the modern paradigm. H.H. Santa Devi had had some spiritual experiences and was a mystic. Even before leaving Delhi, my friend and I had visited her and had interactions with her. After coming to the South, I started seeing them more often. They were old and needed various kinds of help. In the meantime, someone cheated them of their gold and cash by offering to pay higher interest than what the banks offer and walked away with their capital.

Finally, the disciple who was looking after H.H. Santa Devi also passed away. So, I thought I could take care of her in my new house.

Laurie Baker, a famous architect of British origin known for his low-cost housing, which is environment friendly, agreed to build a low-cost place for me with a separate portion for H.H. Santa Devi. She lived with me for the last four-and-a-half years of her life. I had a lady helper who was a cook-cum-caretaker, who also took care of H.H. Santa Devi. I had discussions on spiritual topics with her in my free time. During this period, my father also used to stay with me for six months during the winter.

As mentioned earlier, as a child growing up in a migrant family, I had always longed to have a house in our native place where all the family members could gather. Laurie Baker had helped me build a house where there was enough space for the whole family to get together. This dream of mine was more than fulfilled. Later, my maternal uncle and aunt, who were in Delhi and had no children, decided to stay in my house in the portion built to accommodate H.H. Santa Devi, after she passed away. Thus, in their old age, I was there to take care of them.

Similarly, my paternal uncle and aunt also decided to rent a house near my house. They were old too and opted to come back to their native place. I did not ask them to come to me because I was lonely, as people tended to imagine or assume. They were in no way a burden on me either. They had their own household and cooked their food separately, and did not interfere with my activities, but they had the advantage of sharing my infrastructure if needed. Since they were there, other extended family members visited them, so my ties with the extended family became stronger. Moreover, being in South India, where most of our relatives were, I made it a point to attend family functions, such as marriages and other social and religious ceremonies which we could not participate in when we were in Delhi.

My social philosophy was that one should not lose one's roots. Many migrant families become rootless and lose their identity. I felt that catching up with my roots enriched my life. If I were not single, it would have been difficult to realise some of my dreams. As a single person, I had the *freedom to* make decisions. The presence of all these elderly relatives in and around my house gave me an identity in society. I did not have time to socialise with my neighbours, but through my uncles and aunts, I got connected with them.

The neighbours wondered why, even though I was single, I 'collected' older people around me. It is interesting to see how others view you. For example, a friend remarked, "normally, single women have dogs; you have instead collected old people around you." As I said, I did not collect them around me; they happened to come. And it was not loneliness which prompted me to seek the company of these elderly members of my family. It was more my social philosophy and the search for my roots and identity that were prompting me. When I went abroad, each one of them found others in the family to take care of them and left. Of course, it could also be the maternal instinct in me, which in the absence of marriage got channelled in this way. As mentioned earlier, I had a motherly relationship with my siblings, and maybe here also the maternal instinct in me was getting an outlet.

My Involvement in Women's Studies

The First International Conference for Women took place in Mexico in 1975, and after that, there was a boost given to women's studies. Women's liberation came to be talked of much. After this, the University Grants Commission (UGC) also started the Centre for Women's Studies in most universities. Many women social scientists were encouraged to do research in women's studies. In the 1990s, I became the director of women's studies at the university where I was teaching. Around the same time, the university's women faculty members started a women's forum and chose me as the president.

I wrote a few research articles on women and also guided research in women's studies. However, I was a little concerned that many words had become clichés, such as 'empowerment of women,' 'gender inequality,' 'women's liberation,' and 'patriarchy,' to name a few. I could not flow with the mainstream discourse and had my misgivings about it. Research in women's studies came to be funded liberally, and I found that some of the empirical studies in this area were not up to the mark. I had my differences with the dominant discourse on economic development, and therefore the focus on women and development in this background was not acceptable to me. I expressed some of these views in my articles on women and environment and later published them in a book.

At this time, Professor Arlie Hochschild, a well-known sociologist from the University of California at Berkeley, came to India as a Fulbright Scholar. She visited our centre for women's studies. We had a lot of discussions on the state of the women's liberation movement. I found that they had started a centre for care at Berkeley as they were also feeling that women's liberation should address many more issues – one of them being care. As a social scientist, I had always thought that in Indian society, the family is the most important unit, and no other organisation could replace it. That is why I was committed to the family in my personal life despite having opted out of marriage. I was also not for modernism and did not consider modern society superior to non-modern societies. I found that some people had started discussing these issues in women's studies. Professor Arlie Hochschild's book *The Second Shift*,[1] about working women doing two shifts – one at home and the other in the office – and how capitalism is now exploiting emotions, attracted me as these themes echoed some of my feelings. Therefore, when Professor Arlie Hochschild invited me as a visiting scholar to the Centre for Care Studies in Berkeley, I accepted the invitation and spent three months in Berkeley and eight months at Harvard University with Professor Juliet Schor in her department of women's studies. During the year 2000, I wrote one working paper at Berkeley University, 'Care and Freedom,' and another at Harvard on the wives of H1B visa holders from India in the US working in the IT sector. Most of these women were on H4 dependent visas, meaning they could not take up employment. At this time, I came to

---

[1] Arlie Russell Hochschild, *The Second Shift: Working Parents and the Revolution at Home* (New York: Viking Penguin, Inc., 1989).

know Professor Stephen Marglin of Harvard University, who, along with Frédérique Apffel-Marglin, had edited two books for WIDER (the World Institute for Development Economics Research) studies in development economics, *Dominating Knowledge* and *Decolonizing Knowledge*.[2]

Most of the studies included in these books were critical of the mainstream discourse on economic development. They were addressing some of my concerns with the mainstream discourse on economic development. In my paper 'Care and Freedom,'[3] I questioned the concept of freedom propagated in the mainstream discourse on economic and human development. Later, when I was teaching a course on women and development at the University of Bergen in Norway, I could work out these ideas in my lectures to students from Third World countries. It was heartening to see that students, particularly from Africa, came up with innumerable examples from their own countries and cultures to substantiate what I was saying. I could show them that the dominant discourse on development in general and women's development in particular considered modern society to be superior to non-modern cultures. As the Marglins had brought out in the two volumes published by WIDER mentioned above, this is not tenable. It is here that the meaning of freedom becomes essential. Stephen Marglin had shown that development had become an exercise in coercion. For example, in the transformation of work from home to the factory, there was an attempt to take control of the product and process from the worker.

As a reaction, Amartya Sen wrote his book *Development as Freedom*.[4] I got an opportunity to express some of these ideas as an external consultant at the ILO and the United Nations Social Policy Unit. I

---

2 F. Apffel-Marglin and S.A. Marglin, *Dominating Knowledge: Development, Culture and Resistance* (Oxford: Clarendon Press, 1990) and *Decolonizing Knowledge: From Development to Dialogue* (Oxford: Clarendon Press, 1996).
3 S. Uma Devi, 'Care and Freedom,' Working Paper of the Center for Care Studies, UC at Berkeley (2000).
4 Amartya Sen, *Development as Freedom* (New Delhi: Oxford University Press, 1999).

got encouraged as my ideas and suggestions were received well in both these organisations.

Freedom from, Freedom to, and the Inner Freedom

What I thought and expressed in my paper 'Care and Freedom' in 2000 was not divorced from my life. In a matter of five years, I acted on it. Here, I would like to discuss what type of freedom I was looking for when I chose to remain single. This is important because, as mentioned earlier, I have been sceptical about the mainstream discourse on development and the type of freedom implied in it. Therefore, it was not the pursuit of this type of freedom that led me to choose to remain single. In 'Care and Freedom,' I discuss the three types of freedom – positive, negative, and inner freedom. Positive freedom refers to the *freedom to* while negative freedom refers to *freedom from*. The development enthusiasts talk of negative freedom, but I show that negative freedom is not enough. Even if one gets *freedom from* something, there is no surety that one would get the *freedom to* do what one wants. The development enthusiasts are universalists in their approach. For them, tradition and culture are mostly oppressive. According to them, the oppressive practices of bonded labour, child labour, and customs prevent women from taking up paid work outside the home. Human development achieved by improving human capabilities and functioning, made possible by providing education, better medical care, and a rise in incomes, would increase people's quality of life in developing countries.[5] However, *freedom from* customs and tradition does not ensure the *freedom to* do what one wants. If they were earlier oppressed by custom and tradition, now they get oppressed by the market.

Therefore, the development sceptics ask whether it is necessary to buy a whole package that changes society, polity, culture, and the

---

5 Martha Nussbaum and Jonathan Glover (eds), *Women, Culture, and Development: A Study of Human Capabilities* (New York: Oxford University Press, 1995); Amartya Sen and Martha Nussbaum (eds), *The Quality of Life* (New Delhi: Oxford University Press, 1993).

economy to have economic growth. According to them, development and modernisation have meant industrialisation, urbanisation, and the technological transformation of agriculture. On the political side, this has led to the rationalisation of authority and a rationalising bureaucracy's growth. However, on the social side, it has led to the weakening of hereditary ties and the rise of achievement as the basis of personal advancement.[6] The sceptics also point out that one cannot establish that modernisation has expanded choices. If the modern precludes the possibility of choosing the traditional, then it cannot be considered that the options have expanded.[7]

The nature of the self implied in this discourse of 'development as freedom' is the Western competitive individualist self. It is a self pursuing only individual rights and individual autonomy. Doubts are already being raised about such an individual, who is found incapable of sustaining either a public or a private life.[8] Such individualism is creating a way of life that is neither socially nor individually viable. Both notions of freedom in this discourse of development, viz., in the negative and positive sense (*freedom from* and *freedom to*), look at only the outer freedom and not the inner freedom. It became increasingly clear to me that it is not enough to seek even *freedom to*. The pursuit of outer freedom in the West has led to the creation of the empty self. Being characterised by a pervasive sense of personal emptiness, it has got committed to the values of self-liberation through consumption. As mentioned earlier, my aim of remaining single was not to end up in such an empty self. Such a self, as Cushman says, "is a perfect complement to the economy that wards off stagnation by arranging for the continual purchase and consumption of surplus goods."[9] This self has only one identity, and that is through the work the individual does. If one is not engaged in paid work, one has no identity. Freedom

---

6 Apffel-Marglin and Marglin, op. cit., 1990.
7 Apffel-Marglin and Marglin, op. cit., 1990 and 1996.
8 Robert N. Bellah, Richard Madsen, William M. Sullivan, Ann Swidler, and Steven M. Tipton, *Habits of the Heart: Individualism and Commitment in American Life* (Berkeley: University of California Press, 1984).
9 Philip Cushman, *Constructing the Self, Constructing America* (Reading, MA: Addison-Wesley Publishing Co., 1995), p. 6.

based on disembodied reason alone has led to the depletion of all institutions that formerly protected the 'life world.' There is a lot of rethinking going on about 'family' among the sociologists as well as the feminist scholars in the West. One such attempt is by Barrie Thorne, a sociologist and feminist, showing that feminist positions on the family that devalue its importance have been easily co-opted to serve the interests of the state.[10] The problem is that family of every type has been the location of power and oppression while also being the source of love, care, and nurture. The challenge is to see how this institution can cater to the latter without becoming a tool of oppression. The pursuit of competitive individualism is not the answer because the ultimate aim of ending power and oppression is to move toward an ethic of love and care. Some people have a wrong idea about the single woman, that she is opting out of care and love. This notion is not valid, as one will realise once they understand what is meant by *inner freedom*.

I was getting drawn more and more to the pursuit of *inner freedom*. Very early in life, I had heard that the spiritual goal of life is *moksha*, or the realisation of one's real self, which is liberation or the attainment of *inner freedom*. I had opted to be single to pursue this goal to have the least impediments on this path. As I was growing old, I started becoming increasingly aware that there was less time left to plunge deep into spiritual practice towards this goal. I decided to withdraw from all my secular activities and to spend all my time in spiritual pursuits. I was already 60, and felt this was the right time to begin.

My Spiritual Quest for the 'Real Self'

In fact, in 'Care and Freedom' I had already indicated that "the *advaitic* (non-dualistic) notion of inner freedom might have something to offer even to the West, where alternatives to

---

10 Barrie Thorne, 'Feminist Rethinking of the Family: An Overview,' *Rethinking the Family: Some Feminist Questions*, edited by Marilyn Yalom, pp. 1–24 (New York: Longman, 1982).

competitive individualism are being worked out." Being single has been advantageous in this pursuit of mine. I understood why people renounce worldly activities and take *sanyasa*.

According to Advaita Vedanta, true inner freedom lies in detaching oneself from the false identification with the gross or subtle body and learning to identify oneself as the *Atman*. Therefore, true freedom is internal and not purely external. Unlike the Western individualistic self, the self in this system of philosophy, called the *Atman*, is the cosmic consciousness. It is pure intelligence and is identical to the ultimate metaphysical reality called the *Brahman*. The *Atman* is different from the intellect as the *Atman* or self is the one who illumines, and the intellect is illumined. The *Atman* is changeless and eternal and alone exists. The world of appearances is maintained by each name and form and therefore limited. *Brahman* is infinite and unlimited. By identifying the self falsely with the name and form, or with matter, life, and mind, we limit it and get into bondage. Liberation or freedom is the realisation of the falsity of the identification of the self with matter, life, and mind. Thus, freedom is an inner experience, and the obstacles to it are not external but internal.[11] Restriction of freedom is internal when a higher impulse with which our self has identified is resisted or overpowered by a lower impulse with which our self-identification is still strong. Achieving a free, unhindered play of the higher affords a hearty experience of freedom. Thus freedom is to be attained and enjoyed through an inner process of growth. Such a self or individual is a particular representation of the universal. In fact, the individual, the universal, and the transcendent give the full meaning of existence. There are fewer bondages when one is single. Solitude is essential to practise meditation and to lead a contemplative life.

If in the year 2000 I was theoretically trying to understand the *advaitic* tradition, within five years, in fact, by the end of 2004, I decided to opt for that way of life. As mentioned earlier, I withdrew

---

11 Swami Satprakashananda, *Methods of Knowledge According to Advaita Vedanta* (London: George Allen and Unwin, 1965).

from all secular activities and wanted to lead a contemplative life to realise the *Atman* and *Brahman*. When I started my spiritual practices, I became conscious that I was not sufficiently clear about the path to be traversed. At that time, I had the good fortune of coming in touch with H.H. Swami Paramananda Bharatiji, an *Advaitin Sanyasi*, who initiated me into the study of the Upanishads, Srimad Bhagavad Gita, and the Brahma Sutras known as the Prasthanathraya. Srimad Sankaracharya has written commentaries on all these texts, and these are the texts that all monks and nuns read. I also adopted the life of a Sadhvi (a woman renunciate) and, in the last 15 years, have spent my time only in understanding these texts and practising what is prescribed there. I have not only been learning but imparting it to others who are desirous of learning the same. I keep travelling and sharing my knowledge with others.

Hence the purpose for which I chose to remain single unfolded itself from seeking *freedom to*, towards the search for *inner freedom* and *liberation* – the final goal of life for every Hindu. My life's journey, which began with the search for my roots leading me to my native place, widened as I now understood that my real roots were in *Brahman* and that all the three worlds are my home – *swadeshobhuvanathrayam*. According to the Hindu texts, nothing in life happens accidentally. Each being is born with a purpose. Because Hinduism believes in rebirth, each soul is on its journey towards the attainment of *moksha*; now I understand that whatever has happened to me in my life results from what I have been working for not only in this birth but also in my previous births. I am not the doer; everything is programmed. This does not mean the individual has no role to play. Free will comes to operate in removing one's ignorance about one's true self and therefore getting rid of the sense of doership, enjoyership, and knowership. I am neither the gross nor the subtle body. I am the *Atman*, which is *Brahman*. This is a blissful state. I feel blessed for having led the life of a single woman in an unselfish way, contributing whatever I could to society, and now I feel at peace to pursue my inward journey.

*****

My Journey Towards Wholeness, as a Single Woman

Julian Walker, UK

I married my childhood sweetheart in August 1993. We were both 25 years old. Our wedding photographs show us young and beautiful and obviously in love. Seven years later, the love was still there but our marriage ended in divorce. I have been single now for 20 years, an appropriate time to ask myself why this is and how I feel about my singlehood. To answer those questions, I must first speak about my marriage.

Getting Married, A Dream Come True

My wedding day was the happiest of my life. Everything was perfect – the weather, the marquee, the garden of my parents' Essex farmhouse. In a fitted dress of ivory silk patterned with pale pink and green roses, I elicited a gasp of wonder from my husband-to-be as I walked on my father's arm towards the chapel.

Marriage was what I wanted most, ahead even of my career, and not just marriage, but marriage to him. When we fell in love, I was a clever, competitive, emotionally stunted 17-year-old. Our love gave me a new and wonderful experience of emotional intimacy; we shared secrets and made each other laugh. He was my best friend, and I blossomed in the shelter of his self-confidence and sociability. Through university, whenever crises came, I ran to the safe harbour of his arms, and he always made things better. Our relationship provided the platform for my scholarly success – I could spend my days in the library because I didn't need to spend my nights searching for someone to love and make love to me.

After graduation, we moved to London. My boyfriend and my job were the two best things about me, and when he finally proposed after seven years, I was beyond delighted – certain that I could never find a better man. Our wedding was a culmination, a celebration and vindication that – by some miracle – the man I wanted above all others also wanted me. In front of his mother and the world, he declared his love and promised to cleave to me, forsaking all others. Marriage signalled that our relationship was as important to him as it was to me, ameliorating my feelings of inadequacy.

After my wedding, I could focus my energies on my career. I was surprised, years later, to read bell hooks describe the same satisfaction at entering a committed relationship: "The issue of desire and partnership out of the way (for once I had a male companion, I had proven myself worthy of love – that I was not a failure), I could concentrate on other aspirations."[1] For me, marriage meant him and me, together forever, against the world.

End of the Dream

We divorced because as my husband turned 30, what had started as an itch became an unignorable yearning in him for fatherhood. He needed a child, or the attempt to create one, for our union to be meaningful. I had always seen marriage as an end in itself, not

---

[1] bell hooks, *Communion: The Female Search for Love* (USA: Harper Collins, 2002), p. 143.

a means to an end. It was about deepening and expanding our relationship, including through sexual adventure, not procreation.

Although I had not wanted children at 25 when I married him, I had assumed that a mysterious 'maternal instinct' would overtake me at some point. It never did. In fact, as I matured, my revulsion at the idea of a human parasite in my innards or a baby hanging off my breast or hip deepened. My body exists for my learning and pleasure, not to nurture or satisfy another, except reciprocally. I wanted the sexual love of an adult man, not the unconditional neediness of an infant.

My ex-husband was my best friend and emotional rock. But he tolerated or indulged, rather than rejoiced in, my sexuality. I knew in my gut that becoming the mother of his child would diminish his desire for me, even if it increased his adoration. I was not prepared to make that trade-off.

Why Have I Been Single for 20 Years?

Newly unattached at 32, I sought a new sexual partner for the first time in 14 years. Without quite being conscious of the decision, I gave up believing that any man might replace everything I had cherished and lost with my ex-husband – the tenderness, trust, friendship, conversation, commitment, mutual need. If my marriage hadn't lasted when we had loved one another so desperately, then certainty didn't exist and forever was fatuous.

Through my thirties – now the peak age for women in England and Wales to marry[2] – I sought not permanence but intensity. I never again wanted to be with a man who didn't relish the wild and

---

2 The latest ONS figures for England and Wales show that the average age at marriage of opposite-sex couples was 38 years for men and 35.7 years for women in 2017. Retrieved 27 November 2022. Source: https://www.ons.gov.uk/peoplepopulationandcommunity/birthsdeathsandmarriages/marriagecohabitationandcivilpartnerships/bulletins/marriagesinenglandandwalesprovisional/2017

salacious side of me, so I led with that. If I couldn't have it all, I'd focus on what was uppermost for me, which started but didn't end with sex.

My first lover was an Eritrean wide boy from North London, who approached me at a club called Torture Garden. After that, I chose the role of a predator, not prey. Again, like bell hooks says, "I am not a woman who likes to be seduced. I choose my men; they do not choose me."[3]

I fell in love with an English stripper and the Bosnian son of two generations of muezzins. I fell happily in lust with an Italian hairdresser, a Spanish waiter, an Iranian economist, an Israeli bicycle mechanic, a tattooed personal trainer with a Prince Albert piercing, and with the gentle sidekick of my Serbian cocaine dealer. At the age of 38, I was hopelessly smitten with Alex, a Black Adonis from South Wimbledon 12 years my junior.

In the decade after my divorce, I slept with plenty of beautiful men, pursued relationships that transgressed boundaries of race, class, nationality, and creed. I dressed up to go to specialist adult clubs and enjoyed sex with singles, couples, groups, and multiple partners, at my home or theirs or in the playrooms that fetish clubs provide for that purpose. In none of these relationships was marriage a tenable prospect.

My thirties provided plenty of thrills, and repeated disappointments as lovers who embraced the sex goddess in me retreated from the real woman, with all her contradictory confidence and shame, pride and self-doubt, generosity and self-centredness. Repeatedly, a relationship started with great sex and then, as my feelings deepened and I wanted both to give and receive more, my lover disappeared, sometimes literally. In 2005, my Bosnian boyfriend left our hotel room in Sarajevo to go home and change his underwear; I never saw him again.

---

3 bell hooks, *Wounds of Passion: A Writing Life* (New York: Henry Holt, 1997), p. 199.

The men I attracted and was attracted to proved, time and again, unwilling or incapable of tarrying long enough to allow our relationship to grow. I was both heartbroken and puzzled – why didn't they want more of a good thing, just as I did? I dismissed as patriarchal bullshit the rule that says I should not 'give myself away' so easily. When I fuck a man I desire, I'm giving away nothing; we're exchanging precious gifts. But great sex leads to love, for me, and love lets in a whole new dimension of joy. As James Baldwin wrote, "Without love, pleasure withers quickly, becomes a foul taste on the palate, and pleasure's inventions are soon exhausted. There must be a soul within the body you are holding, a soul which you are striving to meet, a soul which is striving to meet yours."[4] Unfortunately for me, the souls I strove to meet on the whole did not reciprocate.

So, I realise that in my thirties I prioritised other things over a committed relationship. While I believed I was searching for a life partner, how I went about it was ill-conceived and possibly hopeless. I wanted fun and drugs and wild sex, *and* I wanted a relationship to last. I wanted to find a mate who was radically different from me – I eschewed educated, monied, white, middle-class men – and yet I expected him to think and feel just as I did.

As I approached 40, I had to face the fact that my adventuring was getting me no closer to the committed, fulfilling relationship I yearned for. I didn't have to agree with the ideology of female modesty to recognise that my sexual behaviour was causing me pain. I put aside sex and went into therapy. At my therapist's suggestion, I found my way to a 12-step fellowship.[5] I embraced abstinence and began a thoroughgoing, ongoing revision of my ways of relating to the world. And I fell in love with the man I wanted as my second husband.

We had a messy, mutating relationship for the best part of a decade. He was at different times my official partner (for two short periods,

---

4 James Baldwin, *Just Above My Head* (England: Penguin Books, 1994), p. 326.
5 12 step fellowships are self-organising peer support networks for recovery from addiction, originating with Alcoholics Anonymous in Ohio, USA, in 1935.

six years apart); my platonic friend; the man cheating on his girlfriend with me; a flatmate-cum-lover; a live-in fuck buddy; and a 'friend with benefits.' He had no fear of my sexual desire or my androgyny, didn't need me to be 'feminine' in order to prove his masculinity. Nor was he threatened by my intelligence or dismayed by my anger at the unfairness of the world. As a Black British male, he knew all about systems of oppression.

I always wanted a man who could meet me in the dimensions of myself that matter most to me. He was – and is – such a man. But while he meets my soul's deepest need, I don't meet his. Music is the passion that feeds his soul. But a heavy bassline puts my nerves on edge, and I don't like to dance. I could never meet him on the ground which is most sacred to him.

He has needed me for sex and emotional sustenance, and periodically has relied on me financially. But he didn't want my love; at times it was an inconvenience to him. Through him I saw the truth of bell hooks' observation that "Men come to sex hoping that it will provide them with all of the emotional satisfaction that would have come from love."[6]

Society, My Singlehood and Me

On the surface, UK culture doesn't discriminate against single women. 'Why are you single?' is not a question I have ever been asked. No friend or relation has encouraged me to remarry or bemoaned my inability to snag another husband (not in my hearing, at least). I have not encountered discrimination for being divorced. My legal status as single is not something I think about, except when ticking boxes on a form.

But on a deeper level, I am aware of the cultural assumption that for a woman, being married (or in a committed relationship) is

---

6 bell hooks, *The Will to Change: Men, Masculinity and Love* (USA: Washington Square Press, 2004), p. 75.

preferable to being single. And I must confess to having internalised this – I certainly felt myself to be a failure after my divorce. And my feelings today about my singlehood are moderated by my having once been married. I attach value to having once been important enough to a man who was important enough to me that we were wed.

As a feminist, I find problematic the degree to which I've experienced my woman's life to be shaped or made meaningful by the search for love, and I wonder how far we have progressed since Jane Austen's time. I recall my therapist assuring me in my late thirties that I was seeking my soulmate (I wasn't aware that I was, but her saying so made me think I *ought* to be). And female friends to whom I have confessed loneliness or sexual frustration have consoled me not by saying that a single life is a consummation devoutly to be wished but by some version of the formula that if/when I stop searching, love will find me. As I have grown older, this has softened from 'will' to 'may,' but the idea is the same.

The prevalence of divorce may have rocketed since Jane Austen's day,[7] but the underlying assumption remains that, irrespective of career success or individual brilliance, it is romantic fulfilment that matters most to, and for, women. Audre Lorde[8] in 1983 "… we have also been taught that a man acquired was the sole measure of success, and yet they almost never stay."

I sometimes sense female heterosexual friends believe that it's my fault that the men I chose never stayed, because of how I've conducted my sexual/romantic relationships. This reflects a broader cultural assumption that there is something inherently trivial or pathological in a woman pursuing a man for sexual ends. The heroine of the romantic comedy is supposed to fall in the end for

---

7 UK Office for National Statistics (ONS) figures on divorce from 2016 analysed by a British law firm show the average (median) length of a marriage for divorces granted in 2016 was 12.
8 Audre Lorde, *Sister Outsider: Essays and Speeches* (Berkeley: Crossing Press, 1984), p. 167.

the goofy man who has pursued her throughout the film, rather than the heartbreakingly handsome man of her dreams.

Women are meant to 'settle down with' (settle for?) a man who's reliable, works hard, and pays the bills. We are expected to prioritise security over excitement. But why should I take a man I don't desire just because he's reliable or makes me laugh? I pay my own bills and I love laughing most of all with women, over our shared experience, not at the prompting of a man who feels obliged to play the stand-up comedian and expects me to be his audience.

These days I generally keep quiet about my rich sexual history, partly because I anticipate being blamed for still being single. If I'm sexually profligate, goes the patriarchal judgement, of course no decent man will want me. Or he will want me only as a mistress, never as a wife. What I rail against is the – apparent – inability of a man to want me to be both.

Have I Enjoyed Being Single?

For long periods I have been unhappy about being 'single' in the sense of living alone, outside a committed partnership. I have felt that something was missing, not in me but my life. I was often puzzled and sometimes deeply pained as I wondered how far this was the result of chance, of choice (implicit or otherwise), or a consequence of some fundamental unfitness in me. I sometimes joked that, surely, I was perfect heterosexual girlfriend material: I had my own flat, my own money, I liked sex, *and* I liked football. How were men not crawling over broken glass to woo me?

I have often judged myself for my inability to keep a man, belittling the many successes and joys of my life and dwelling instead on men I have loved and lost. Once again, I find solace in bell hooks' penetrating feminist critique of this female preoccupation with love. She shows how women become obsessed with love as a way of securing from without rather than within the value and approval that we seek. "Our obsessions about love begin not with the first crush or the first fall.

They begin with that first recognition that females matter less than males, that no matter how good we are, in the eyes of a patriarchal universe we are never quite good enough." She goes on to say "This is a female's first lesson in the school of patriarchal thinking and values. She must earn love. She is not entitled. She must be good to be loved. And good is always defined by someone else..."[9] This idea brings the elusive prospect that if I could locate my definition of 'good' within myself, then I could stop waiting for another's validation – I could be content with singlehood, if not always with celibacy.

How Do I Feel Today Being Single?

I might believe in my head that a woman needs a man like a fish needs a bicycle[10] but I wish someone would tell my heart. I retain vestiges of the stubborn girlchild's fantasy that if I grow sufficiently as a person, a happy and healthy relationship will be the inevitable result or reward.

I find this fantasy unhelpful. I know it is rooted in social conditioning and fertilised by my psyche's penchant for projection. I know that it smothers my efforts to find emotional and spiritual sustenance within. So I take conscious steps to ensure the fantasy does not abide with me daily. On any given day, I feel proud, grateful, and comfortable being single. I enjoy my independence and my own company. I look at my married female friends and I don't want their lives. I certainly don't want their husbands. I am part of the demographic – single, childless women – who are apparently the happiest subgroup in the population.[11]

I love living alone in a space that meets my own requirements, knowing that if I come to need something different, I can up and

---

9 hooks, *Communion*, p. xi.
10 Attributed to Australian feminist Irina Dunn and subsequently popularised by Gloria Steinem.
11 Suzanne Moore, *Guardian*, 27 May 2019. Retrieved 25 November 2022. Source: https://www.theguardian.com/commentisfree/2019/may/27/marriage-children-women-happy-science-markers-success-paul-dolan

move at will. I love sleeping alone and waking up alone, and the longer I do it, the more I enjoy it. I like not having to negotiate the minutiae of daily life with another person. As I strengthen my spirituality, my need for solitude deepens.

Today I feel content as a single woman – better than resigned, if not quite triumphant. I don't feel socially inferior. Nor do I feel incapacitated or lacking agency and influence in the world. And yet, I can't say that I have *chosen* this status. I can see how it has resulted from the choices I have made. But the fact is, if I had got what I wanted from life thus far, I would not now be alone. I make peace with that by resting in humility and gratitude, recognising that life outcomes are never something we can demand, only welcome gratefully if they fall into our lap.

Gifts of Being Single

Some years ago, I told my ex-husband that his leaving me was the act for which I most admired him and for which I'm most grateful. His leaving gave me the freedom to explore my sexuality, energetically and unapologetically. I rejoice in the fact that there's nothing I dreamed of as a lustful teenager or frustrated married woman that I have not now experienced. Except perhaps the final fantasy that would have been fulfilled had my last lover also wanted me as his wife.

Being single, I have been free to explore the world. I could take the risk in 2001 to quit the senior civil service and set up my own business, knowing that nobody would suffer but me if I failed. My first international contract was in Kabul, and since 2003 I have worked in Ramallah, Juba, Tripoli, Tunis, Kigali, and Freetown. I could not (or would not) have done all that if I had a man at home worrying about me or had been expected to run a household or expend the emotional labour that women are expected to give to male partners. I have been able to pursue work meaningful to me rather than feeling pressure to rise the corporate ladder or earn a lot to sustain my partner's lifestyle.

I have had the time, resources, and emotional energy to pursue my interests without guilt and the complex negotiations required of women in relationships. I never have to convince a sceptical or insecure partner that my personal growth doesn't threaten him or argue over the ways I choose to be frugal or profligate with my money.

I have been free to devote considerable resources to my inner work. I have invested in extensive and intensive personal development, including an 18-month Gestalt OD and leadership programme conducted across three continents. I have had time to devote to my writing, thinking, and practice as a white intersectional feminist and antiracist.

I know that some women grow and develop within a committed relationship, but that was never going to be my journey. In a sexual partnership, I find it difficult to occupy the middle ground between controlling everything or silencing myself. When I was married, I was insular and resistant to trying anything new (except sexually). As a newly single woman, I took motorbike lessons and trained as a Samaritans volunteer. I found a wider circle of friends. Being single, I connected to a wider universe outside my white, middle-class world and eventually built a more solid sense of self in the process.

What's precious to me is not just the people I have met but the person I have become on this journey. I have travelled the world and travelled deep within myself. I am able to hear other people's pain or shame or fear without flinching. As a friend and as a sponsor in my 12-step fellowship, I'm pretty much unshockable. I'm not brave physically, but I have emotional courage, and people choose to confide in me, not because I'm especially kind or wise, but because they know I can hold the space for whatever they need to share, without judgement. I can face the truth about myself and I can face it in other people.

But for all my pride in my independence, I feel somehow lacking or unfinished as a human being in certain contexts. Not that as a woman I need a man to complete me, but that I might be a fuller, richer person with the learning that comes from sustaining, and being sustained within, an intimate relationship.

Lessons from My Singlehood

This feeling of inadequacy leads me to inquire what special gifts I might have to offer as a woman and practitioner by dint of my long-term singleness. I model what it is to have the courage to stand alone. I am not afraid to differentiate or stand in opposition to a group to be true to myself. I do not fear the group's rejection since I need their approval less than I need my own integrity.

It took too long, but I have learned through being single that it's my responsibility to get my needs met, to manage my feelings, and to make myself happy. It's nobody's job but mine, not my husband's or my mother's or my lover's or my friend's. Being single has helped me learn that I have to find my own answers in life, make my own meaning. If I'm living for somebody else (or to win somebody else's approval), I'm missing the point.

I am not suggesting that only those who are single learn these lessons, but I believe I could not have grown towards wholeness without an extended period alone. I have found it slow and painful work to recognise and accept my emotional vulnerabilities without shutting down, cutting myself off, or mocking or insulting myself. I can still experience my needs – for love, connection, tenderness – as overwhelming and somehow repellent. But after years of inner work, I can look at myself face-on without flinching. I can look without contempt at my unresolved pain and hold that wounded self in compassion. I feel in my gut that this would not have been possible, *for me*, in the context of a loving relationship.

I know how easily I 'project' what I feel or fear onto those closest to me; I know how easy it is for me to focus on fixing another person or to blame them for not loving me enough. If I had another escape route, I would take it rather than face the hard task of accepting and loving myself. Repeatedly in relationships, I have subcontracted to my lover the emotional work of providing the acceptance I crave.

My Experience of Writing My Journey

I hoped that writing this piece would enable me to see myself more as the captain of my soul, not a hapless, helpless woman tossed on the seas of fate. I wanted to ditch my old narrative that I was abandoned again and again by men who lacked the courage to deal with a strong, sexual woman. That narrative denies my agency and limits my ability to learn and change. It has fuelled my anger at men, which is inconvenient given that I am stubbornly heterosexual and will need some day to open my heart to a man if I'm to have another chance at love.

More damagingly, that story has fed a disabling sense of unworthiness and bewildered heartbreak in me. In the process of writing this piece, I spent some anguished days asking myself, why did none of them want me? But I can never answer this question. Their motivations are opaque to me and actually none of my business. If the sad and angry child in me wants to know why, my job is to love and soothe her, not try answering her question. Because her question misses the point: the more interesting question is why I didn't want me.

Has my narrative changed? Yes and no. The anger and pain of rejection have diminished but not yet disappeared. Once or twice, I experienced debilitating sadness and barely containable rage and put this manuscript aside as those feelings overwhelmed me. Between the first and second drafts, I read bell hooks' *Communion: The Female Search for Love*.

Not for the first time, hooks gave me a theoretical framework to understand my own experience. What resonated most with me was her critique of the trope of 'women who love too much' – a category into which I might have placed myself. She writes, "The irony… is that most of us were not loving too much; we were not loving at all. What we were was emotionally needy, desperate for the recognition… that would prove our worth, our value, our right to be alive on the planet."[12]

Conclusion

Reviewing my single woman's journey, I have no regrets. I certainly don't regret being childless. Nor do I regret the end of my marriage or the adventures which followed. I might still wish at times that my last lover had wanted me as I wanted him, but I don't regret spending as long as I did in that relationship, hoping that his feelings would change. It takes as long as it takes to recognise that one deserves more.

On a good day, I love myself and I love my life. On a bad one, I count my many blessings. On balance, I think my singlehood has enhanced rather than diminished my life, providing the context for me to learn both what I need and that taking responsibility for getting my needs met is not a selfish thing but a responsible, loving way of being.

I don't know whether I will remain single for the rest of my life; it would be no tragedy if I did. There may yet be a second husband: in the past decade, marriage rates for women aged 65 plus have increased in England and Wales by an enormous 89%.[13] Maybe the sexual animal in me, an unrepentant lover of men and men's bodies, need not be interred quite yet.

*****

12 hooks, *Communion*, p. xv.
13 Source: https://www.ons.gov.uk/peoplepopulationandcommunity/birthsdeaths andmarriages/marriagecohabitationandcivilpartnerships/bulletins/marriages inenglandandwalesprovisional/2017

Single Woman in a Men's World

Anney George, India[1]

Shri Ratan Tata, one of the noblest and the richest industrialists of India, has been frequently asked, "Why are you single?" His answer has been, "I came seriously close to getting married four times and each time, I backed off in fear or for one reason or another. Each occasion was different, but in hindsight, when I look at the people involved, it wasn't a bad thing what I did. I think it may have been more complex had the marriage taken place."[2]

I too, have been asked the same question. However, unlike Mr. Tata, I came close to getting married only twice. And, unlike him, I am not yet 80.

I also notice and understand the different nuances of the question when it is asked of Mr. Tata and when it is asked of me. Mr. Tata is asked this question because he is rich, handsome, and successful. It is an anomaly for a man of his stature to remain single. Therefore, when he is asked this question, there is an element of pleasant

---

[1] This is a pseudonym.
[2] 'Came close to getting married four times: Ratan Tata,' *Times of India*, 2011. Retrieved 27 November 2022. Source: https://timesofindia.indiatimes.com/business/india-business/came-close-to-getting-married-four-times-ratan-tata/articleshow/7972929.cms?from=mdr#:~:text=In%20an%20interview%20to%20CNN,for%20one%20reason%20or%20another%E2%80%9D

disbelief. On the other hand, when I am asked this question, there is an element of subtle pity; certain doubt in my femininity, in my being a 'real' woman, in my capacity to 'attract a man;' and ultimately a subtle rejection of my whole existence per se. The reason for all these perceptions lies in my social, political, and financial circumstances.

I lost my father in the year 2006. I have no brother, boyfriend, or husband, and – the cherry on top of the cake – I have been a freelance content writer, translator, and editor since the year 2013, which means no stable job and no steady income. In my social interactions, I have sensed that people often have this curiosity about my life and me. They have this question in their eyes, if not on their lips: how can I, a middle-class woman with no stable income, nor a man of her own by her side, possibly survive in the world, which is predominantly ruled by men and money? This question then translates into many adjectives: brave, failure, arrogant, irresponsible, free bird, too individualistic, too independent, and so on. All of these are rooted in different perceptions.

I am tempted to quote Bella Depaulo's article 'Why Are You Still Single?' in which Depaulo herself quotes Jessica Francis Kane's novel *Rules for Visiting Friends.* This is a conversation between May, who is 40 and has always been single, and her once-close friend Vanessa, who is married. It goes as follows:

> "Vanessa asks May, 'Can I be brutally honest?' May says OK. Vanessa then asks, 'Why are you still single?' May responds without hesitation: 'Why are you married?'"

De Paulo comments:

> "That might strike you as a snide remark or a clever come-back. And it can be used in that way, though I would modify it a bit to parallel the question May was asked, 'Why are you still married?'"[3]

---

3 Bella DePaulo, '"Why Are You Still Single?": Here's the Best Way to Answer' (2019). Retrieved 22 November 2022. Source: https://www.psychologytoday.com/us/blog/living-single/201907/why-are-you-still-single-heres-the-best-way-answer

Yes, the May within me also asks the same question to so many Vanessas out there in the world.

Why Am I Still Single at 40?

It is as simple as this: I am yet to meet somebody meant for me. In our society, the expectations of getting married start from a very tender age. In my household, however, it was complex. I was not expected to get married. My parents were kind of relaxed with my resolve to remain single. My decision was based on their toxic married life, and they knew it quite well, and so they and their extended family endorsed my resolve in their hearts and minds, if not socially or politically.

However, my heart indeed yearned for a solid romantic partnership in the form of marriage. So, this toxic absorption of the energies in my home and the yearnings of my heart often collided and resulted in a couple of toxic relationships with people who were never meant for me. Growing up in a dysfunctional family, I had developed serious emotional blind spots that proved lethal at every level in my life.

I did and do want a stable, romantic relationship within the institution of marriage, despite having grown up in a dysfunctional family. Because I've seen and absorbed what marriage should not be, perhaps I know better what it should be. For me, marriage is a union of mind, heart, and body – a true Yoga. And, therefore, run-of-the-mill reasons to marry never made sense to me. These 'popular' reasons and my views are as follows:

- *A woman should marry at a 'proper' age to have regular, protected sex and children.*

    Having regular and protected sex may help to an extent in increasing the overall quality of life, but ultimately, it is not a reason enough for me to marry. I enjoy not the act of sex per se but the volcano of emotions involved in it. If I do not feel wanted, safe, desirable, and respected in the other's life, it does not make sense to me to marry just for the sake of regular protected sex.

- *A woman must marry at a 'proper' age so that she can adjust to a new environment.*

I believe we need to adjust everywhere and at every stage of life, irrespective of age. The negative connotations attached to the word 'adjustment' are naïve. We all adjust regardless of our marital status or age. This too is not a good enough reason for me to marry.

- *A woman must marry at a 'proper' age so that she does not feel lonely after a certain age.*

When I hear this from people as their reason to get married, I cannot help but smile. As I mentioned earlier, I grew up in a dysfunctional family that looked like the perfect one on the surface. So, I know what it is to be lonely even when you're in a family. Could this be the reason for me to get married? The answer is obviously 'no.'

- *What would people say?*

This is yet another comic reason. In my life, I've experienced people commenting on anything and everything, no matter what I do. For example, if I talk to them the way they want to be talked to, they would ask me why I'm talking in that way. If I don't talk to them, they would ask me why I'm not talking to them. This is hilarious and has taught me one thing: let people say what they want to say. Try to focus on your centre and do whatever is necessary. Hence, people's perceptions, thankfully, are never my motivators to marry.

- *How would you cope with social realities?*

Everyone has to learn to cope with all kinds of reality. In my case, I'm learning to cope with many social realities that are indeed heartbreaking – for example, unequal pay and discriminatory treatment at the workplace due to my gender and marital status.

So, these common reasons to marry have never attracted me. Once I find the right person who shares the same vibes as me, there would be nothing that could stop us getting married, I reckon.

A single life until the age of 40 indeed has created some interesting experiences. Some of these experiences I share below. They are reflections of the patriarchal world that we live in.

Travelling and Eating in Restaurants Solo

In October 2019, I travelled alone to Pondicherry after a gap of almost ten years since my last solo travel. I was full of anxiety and self-doubts. But, as Mother's Grace would have it, I had the most beautiful and enriching travel experience, including the one I want to share here.

I wanted to eat in a small, cosy restaurant called Dilliwaala6 in the 'Whitetown' area of this cosmopolitan tourist place. However, when I went there for dinner, I realised that the restaurant was full. Still, the owner tried to accommodate me. He showed me a couple of seats where there was no air conditioner, and it was difficult to fit in. He was staring at me as if I would 'adjust.' I said I would not eat in a place that is too hot. So, he finally gave me the place which had four chairs. I ordered one roti and vegetable kolhapuri (an Indian vegetarian delicacy). The quantity was too large for a single person, and I could not eat it all. Then, the waitress asked me about the food experience. I said that I had really enjoyed the food, but it would have been better if they could also serve for one person. It would prevent waste of food, and it would be reasonable on my pocket too. To which the owner said, "Madam, this is a family restaurant."

I truly felt that I was unwelcome there because they did not expect a single woman to dine alone. And I admit, there was nobody else in the restaurant at that time who was eating alone. So, yes, I did come across as an anomaly again. I indeed laughed inwardly at this comic existential predicament of my life. And, it is not just about travelling. In the city where I live, I have not heard of any restaurant which is singles friendly. I have read that in one European country, they have a restaurant only for single people. This is a big socio-political statement. It not only validates but also welcomes people who want to experience eating solo.

Going to Movies Solo

Well, this is not that big a deal nowadays. However, an incident indeed made me feel a bit awkward about watching a movie solo. I went there to buy a ticket and insisted on getting a centre seat. However, the person at the ticket counter requested that I buy a ticket for a side seat. He reasoned that if a group of people came to watch the movie, my seat would not be an 'obstacle' in their group movie-watching experience. If I detach myself from the episode, there is nothing bizarre about this argument. But I certainly felt that, just because I was single, I was required to compromise on my desired viewing experience despite my purchasing power.

Attending Social Functions

This too, turns out to be unpleasant as well as comical sometimes. Let me explain this by giving an example. I am invited to a friend's social event, such as her own wedding or her child's birthday party or her sibling's wedding, or any other function. I attend it solo. Now, when I go there, people seem to find it very strange that I can simply enjoy being myself in a big social gathering without any company from someone of 'my own.' This feeling of strangeness perhaps sometimes makes them over-attentive to me. I enjoy being paid attention. However, when I realise that the reason for the extra attention is not their genuine desire to spend time with me, this certainly pains me. And, even when they appreciate me by saying things like "You are so calm, even if alone," "You are so brave that you can attend such events alone," "You are so comfortable being alone," etc., it pinches at times. It does make me feel as if I am doing something strange and heroic by not having an exclusive man by my side. My heart questions: why is it so and why is doing this not seen as natural? What would it change for them if I had my own man? It can make a difference to my life at some level, but how can their decision to be with me be shaped by the absence of a man in my life? Why should their being with me stem from a sense of obligation and not from a sense of joy and pleasure? Why would I be pitied, or why would someone be concerned about me, just for not having my own exclusive man at someone's function? They have already invited me knowing full well my marital status, haven't they?

In spite of such questions, I just accept their company because I perfectly know that I cannot change how they think or their reasons for being with me. As long as I can enjoy the function, I have learnt not to mind. When I recall some of the social functions that I attended with my family and some other family friends, I realise that even if people are with their own man or woman, they need someone's company, whereas I can comfortably eat on my own and talk to people (or not talk to them, for that matter) irrespective of whether I am with my family or alone. But then, nobody asks those people, "Why are you so anxious even if you are with your man or a woman?" If there is a perception that a single woman is anxious attending a social function solo, then it goes by default that couples or people with a company are at ease, doesn't it? ;)

So, yes, being single does mean that my social interactions become limited, especially with my extended family. However, I do meet a couple of friends, connect, and socialise. This is usually a one-on-one meeting, and it is indeed enriching and refreshing, unlike the embarrassing social functions I experience either with family or with a group of friends.

Shopping Solo

Well, this is somewhat tricky – and I admit that I need some company for this. I am learning to do small shopping on my own, though. There was a time when I actually got scared going shopping alone, especially for clothes. I am fortunate enough to have a couple of friends who help me with my fears of going shopping all alone. But this aspect of being single did make me feel too vulnerable at times.

Conversations in Personal and Professional Spaces

This too used to be a bit funny. The fun starts when I am expected to engage in a kind of social communication that I am not normally exposed to. I've been working from home for almost seven years now. Things have become all the more difficult, as I don't have any socio-political office story to share with people. Also, since I'm single, I do not have any common, conventional stories of a 'family.' What I have to share, nobody is interested in or able to relate to. And that results in either unwanted pieces of advice or total disbelief, creating an enormous sense of disconnection.

During these seven years working as a freelancer, I happened to have a short stint of almost nine months working in an international NGO, for which I had previously been working as a consultant. It was during this period that I had this distinct realisation about different professional spaces. Most women of my age, or even those younger than me, are mothers. They have issues with children and in-laws. So when I needed to interact with them during leisure time in the office, I did feel like an alien from within. There is this sense of displacement as if I do not belong to their world. It's not that I cannot talk on these subjects. In fact, I do so with great care and concern. However, sometimes, I hear statements like "You won't understand it as you do not have an experience of this," or "You are so lucky that you do not have any responsibilities." It seems that often those who live a life expected of them by their culture don't seem to have the basic wisdom that all kinds of life situations involve their own positives and negatives.

In such conversations with people, I do experience that they often choose to look down upon me, pity me, or at times, label me as brave or a failure. At the same time, I have met people who confided in me that they cannot live 'alone' like me, which is why they got married and remained so. I also have relatives telling me this. I have a cousin brother who got divorced almost 20 years ago. His sole reason to remarry was that all his friends had children, and that made him panic. This sense of panic and being less than his peers made him remarry. Both my ex-brother-in-law and sister also told me once that they could not imagine being all 'alone' like me, which was the reason they did not divorce. However, they finally divorced in spite of their fears of being alone. What is quite evident from such conversations is that people do know and live the hollowness of their marital life. My only question is, if I can understand their decision and life circumstances to remain married or to get divorced, and take it as it is, why can't they behave naturally with me without labelling me either brave or failure?

Hence, when conversing with people who live as per the defined socio-cultural structure, I also feel a lack of emotional representation of my outer or inner world. It does feel like my experiences, feelings, thoughts, and sensibilities of being who I am simply do not find any space in the 'mainstream' dialogues of the world, and therefore, I do feel left out at times. Lack of emotional representation also means a lack of socio-political representation and lack of adequate socio-political power. This then manages to create an acute sense of separation.

Being Single Means Available for Anything or Anybody

I've experienced this aspect of being single on two fronts: professional and personal. At times, when somebody is sick or someone needs some other help in the family, I used to be called for help or assistance. The reason was not that I was their favourite or they had a great connection with me. The reason for asking my help was the perception that since I am single and don't have any 'responsibility,' I'm absolutely free and available. This used to happen even if I had a job that demanded almost 12 hours of my day.

I had to quit my last job with an international NGO due to a health emergency. After I quit the job, one of my former colleagues asked me for a sexual relationship without emotional investment. He messaged me in the middle of the night, saying since he hadn't had sex with his wife for the last 13 months, and he was horny and attracted to me because I am a curvy woman. The boss of the same NGO also made subtle, indirect advances such as requesting that I be his friend even if I am no longer an employee; chatting about personal things; inviting me to his home, and even sympathising with me when I shared this incident of being asked for sexual favours by one of his subordinates. All these things happen because they took my openness and vulnerability for granted. They thought that since I have 'different' ideas of the world, I'm just available for them for anything. My having some perceived different opinions about many things of the world gets translated into being available to them.

This type of thing has happened with so many men. If I write something or speak something, men infer that I am simply a woman who does not believe in commitment and responsibility. Such men included so-called intellectuals, spiritual people, simpletons, poor men, rich men, religious men, atheists, CEOs, and their subordinates. These men were married, single, or in a relationship. Though I might have taken a tough stand against all these and spoken harsh language to protect myself, it has indeed caused me great pain, not just emotional and spiritual, but also professional and financial. I had to let go of some contacts that could have been beneficial for my work. It also meant the loss of a great possibility of a very healthy and enriching friendship. I have hardly come across a powerful, well-connected man who genuinely wanted to help me boost my career (while some of them approach with such promises) or to be genuine friends with me.

My boss in the last job promised to buy the first insurance from me when I passed an insurance agent examination after quitting the job. He said that he was not doing any favour to me but only fulfilling his duty as a friend. Those words of his indeed melted my heart at that point in time. He also promised to invest in my business plan. But the moment I refused to stay at his home for the night or to help him cook every weekend, he would not talk about my business or my business plan. All he was interested in was me cooking at his home during the weekend or staying at his home during the night. He wanted me to come to his house even after he came back from Mumbai after a historic lockdown. Not for a single moment would he ask about my work situation or life situation. All he wanted was for me to travel there, spending 125 rupees for transport, cook for him, hug him, and have sex with him. Since he realised that none of this would happen, he tried to maintain contact by asking trivial things constantly during the day, like "How are you?" "Why do you sound so distant?" "Can you put me in touch with All India Radio?" It is at that time that I shut him off from my life, letting go of my hope to get some work through him.

When I pondered over this, I realised that my inherent softness, genuineness, purity, vulnerability, and warmth attract men such as him, as I am always soft-spoken and cordial to them. But when they realise that even if I am soft, vulnerable, emotional, sensitive, and warm to them, I am absolutely not available to serve their bogus fantasies and that I cannot be taken advantage of at any point of time, they perceive me as a threat to their sense of supremacy. In this case, and a couple of my other experiences, men in power often think that my admiration for them would naturally translate into sexual favours. When this is expected of me, I stop all communication even if they apologise or want to be in touch, as I do not trust them anymore.

This brings to the surface a very painful fact that even though there are stringent safeguarding policies for women to protect them from sexual exploitation at work, there are subtle things that are impossible to address through such policies. One of the most important among them is, can you stop people from thinking of a single working woman as an object of their sexual gratification? Can you make them stop thinking of single women as their prey? Perhaps not. For example, my boss, whom I respected a lot, and who wanted me to stay overnight at his home, was part of creating an anti-sexual-harassment policy for that institution in which I had been working. The only way out for women is to be emotionally tougher without losing their inherent openness, vulnerability, and femininity. How to do this is not taught in any university or school or family. This is something we, the women, need to learn along the way to survive in a dignified and graceful way.

Relating to My Own Self

Well, in the words of the Mother, all these things are called vital forces. They do affect you, and they do torture you like hell. Having grown up on the staple diet of 'not being enough' has indeed caused me deep wounds emotionally. But, at the same time, 'not being enough' and 'being single' have pushed me to question my own legitimacy in this world where being a single woman is indeed a taboo. This self-enquiry has made me realise that being alone and being single are not related. Being alone is essentially a mental phenomenon, and we are all in it whether we are married or single. Perhaps the horrible coronavirus pandemic that we are all facing right now is teaching us the same thing the hard way. I've seen in my own family as well as in the world out there that there are thousands of married people who are alone or lonely in their mind and heart and therefore need more help than me, who is socially single. It is only that the world at large has been kinder and protective to those who are married. For me, it always has harsh or dubious questions.

Hence, yes, it has undoubtedly been a lonely life for long, and a tough one at that. At the same time, I have been blessed with my mother's strong financial and social support, my wonderful friends, and my work so far, even if its highest potential has not yet been realised. There is no denying that there are regrets, sorrows, and frustrations that being single brings in a world obsessed with marriage and things associated with it. One of my ways to make peace with these frustrations is to measure their scale against reality as it is. I have realised that both the sorrows of being single and the joys of being married are blown out of proportion. Both these sorrows and joys are essentially perceptions. Since I realised this, I have been learning to experience life from a more centred, sorted, deeper, and authentic space. I would say I have come a long way as far as my inner space is concerned. And the journey continues.

The World of My Dreams

I dream of a world where the proprietor of that restaurant in Pondicherry would be heard saying this to me or, for that matter, to any other single woman: "Welcome Ma'am. We surely have many delicacies at good prices that serve the single person too. You can also have your cosy area at our place. And, all this makeover is the result of a precious suggestion given to us by our very special guest who visited us ten years ago."

I dream of a world where powerful, well-connected men or women, for that matter, help single women climb the ladder rather than just seeing them as an object of their unfulfilled sexual or power fantasies.

I dream of a world where a single woman is not continuously asked why she is single and is not stared at when she goes out alone in the world.

On the personal front, my single life so far has given me an opportunity to look deeper into so many realities which otherwise would not have been possible to penetrate. Therefore, I am thankful for my life. I cannot say if the struggles are worth it or not. They only are, I reckon. The only thing worth doing in life, I have realised after so long, is to accept oneself and one's life the way they are, wholeheartedly. The only way ahead for me is to make absolute peace with whatever is, and for that matter, whatever is not, with who I am and who I am not. And I am sure blessings are always there.

*****

My Non-traditional Journey

Deborah Howard, USA

My journey to being single has not been a straightforward one; I never intended to be single. However, after a six-year marriage, I became divorced and have been single now for 20 years.

Marriage

As a young girl, I never had dreams or fantasies about walking down an aisle in a white dress. Marriage was not even something I contemplated until I was in my late thirties. My main focus had always been on my career and being financially independent. It never occurred to me to think of having someone else in my life who would 'take care of me' financially. Nonetheless, having a man in my life was something I considered critical to my happiness and essential for me to feel whole and complete.

My need to have a man in my life was less about conforming to society's mores than about the feelings I experienced as a result of childhood sexual abuse. I was molested by my father at a young age. This experience has impacted every part of my life. It was not until decades after this experience, years of therapy and finally writing a memoir, *Mystery of Memory*,[1] about it, that I became fully aware of just how many ways this trauma has shaped my life and my worldview.

Being violated at a young age, by the very person who was responsible for my safety and well-being, and being completely unable to defend myself, left me with deep-seated feelings of vulnerability and powerlessness. For many years before I got married, I felt anxious around my father unless I had a boyfriend accompany me on visits. I believe that on some unconscious level, I felt I needed a 'protector' with me when I was around my father.

Even at a young age, I knew what my father was doing to me was wrong. What I did not understand, however, was that it was not my fault. I internalised feeling responsible for what happened, as well as being worthless and unlovable as a result. Unconsciously, I concluded that there was something defective and sullied about me as a person for this to have happened. I spent decades feeling helpless, worthless, and unlovable. Having a man in my life had been a major strategy to keep these feelings at bay. Only then could I feel safe, protected, worthy, and lovable. Being single felt frightening; having a man was essential.

Once I was in a relationship, if anything went wrong, I felt responsible. I would turn myself inside-out trying to say or do things differently to make the relationship work. My focus was never on the man's behaviour, but on what I might be doing to induce it or could do to change it. While the focus was on myself, it wasn't to create a life for myself of freedom and expansion; it was with the sole purpose of ensuring that the relationship would work so as to quell feelings of worthlessness.

Having a man was vital, being married was not. In my late thirties, after having been in a relationship with a man for four years, being married in a formally committed relationship became attractive to

---

1 Deborah Howard, *Mystery of Memory: Telling My Truth and Standing My Ground* (New York: Guiding Change Consulting, 2017).

me. During this four-year relationship, we did not live together, but I co-parented his young son from a prior relationship. The marriage was less about succumbing to traditional societal mores than about wanting to feel that my partner was making a real commitment to me.

My marriage itself was completely non-traditional, starting with my conditional "yes" to the proposal. The conditions were: "no cooking and no more kids." Just as marriage had never been a childhood dream of mine, neither was having children. In fact, I never intended to have any until I experienced and enjoyed parenting my husband's son (now my son as well) and decided to have another child. My daughter was born in my first year of marriage.

The marriage ceremony was also non-traditional: I wore a rose-coloured dress; the wedding took place in the morning in the suite of a hotel with fewer than ten people present; my 'maid of honour' was my dearest friend, who was a man; the 'best man' was our son; the 'reception' was brunch at a nearby restaurant; and there was no honeymoon – my then husband and I went back to work the following day.

I didn't feel hampered by social norms in general. Many of my life choices have not been in line with the boundaries established by society. I've travelled and lived on my own, within and outside of my home country, the USA. When I got married, my marriage was interracial. Then, after getting divorced, I maintained physical custody of both children and welcomed my ex-husband's various significant others into my home as an extended family. Living outside of social norms has never been a challenge for me. What was essential for me was to live in alignment with my own values.

Having said all that, my marriage did in many ways follow social norms. I ended up doing a lot of cooking (despite the condition I set when my ex-husband proposed); I handled all the cleaning and laundry; did most of the homework help; and attended most parent–teacher meetings on my own. I undertook all of this almost unconsciously; it was not demanded of or thrust upon me. I did, however, push back against certain social norms of which my then husband could not let go. Even though I was the one bringing in a higher and more stable income, my husband acted as the breadwinner, with his work taking priority over all else. In fact, many of our fights were over his spending time at work that I would have preferred him to spend with the children.

Becoming Single

My marriage had troubles from the start. Even though I felt constrained, stifled, and living small, it took me years to take the step of initiating my divorce. By the time I started divorce proceedings, I had come to the realisation that if I wasn't spending my emotional and mental energy focusing on what I might be doing wrong and what I needed to do differently to make the marriage work, I could focus on what I needed to live a satisfying life. Getting a divorce felt liberating for me.

Once divorced, however, I found myself with no choice but to finally confront my feelings of being vulnerable, worthless, and unlovable. Being able to love myself and feel safe on my own took time. This was, hands down, one of the biggest challenges I faced in my life. Along with therapy and coaching, it took an intentional focus on self-development and growth.

Coming to See Being Single as a Social Identity

I had not seen my being single as a significant part of my identity until co-facilitating a workshop on the topic of single women. It all started on a sunny morning in Avignon, France. My colleagues Uma and Heather and I had just attended a writing retreat and were spending time together before returning to our respective homes. While we sat outside enjoying breakfast, Uma mentioned her long-time desire to have a workshop for single women in India and write a book about their journeys.

As someone always ready to jump at the chance to do creative work with colleagues I love and respect, not to mention to work outside the US, I immediately said I'd love to be involved. Uma may not have originally seen someone like me, a woman who had been married for a number of years and had children, as fitting within the category of single women, but she was willing to broaden the criteria to include me.

While I definitely saw myself as being a single woman, I saw being single as more like a fact in my life than as a significant social identity. Nonetheless, I was excited to explore it with other single women. In agreeing to work with Uma and Heather on this project, I had no expectations other than to co-create, learn, and connect with other single women. I didn't realise at that time the significance to me of my identity as a single woman.

I left the week-long workshop with awe for Uma, having seen the significance and impact of the social identity of being single. I felt comfortable in my singleness but had not realised that many of the ways I am impacted by being single were below my consciousness. Uma, however, had clearly seen the impact on members of this social identity group as well as how important it is that society changes its view and treatment of single women.

By the end of the workshop, I felt a kinship with the other participants, a strong sense of group belonging, and an understanding of the impact on me and others of being single. Moreover, I came to recognise the need that had been so clear to Uma, to surface and focus consciously on this social identity group and its experiences.

Becoming Conscious of Being Single as a Social Identity

During the workshop, one of the first things I became conscious of was the way society puts people in boxes based on their marital status. When Uma, Heather, and I originally planned the workshop, we intended to have participants form groups for exploration based on the categories of being divorced, always single, or widowed.

Unconsciously, we had taken on the categories in which society puts us. The participants, however, did not want to be grouped this way. What did it matter how we came to be single? It was at this point that I realised that those categories were all centred around marriage as if that were the norm and all other categories were relative to that norm. I understood only then why, whenever I completed such things as applications, surveys, or doctor's questionnaires and had to choose between checking 'divorced' or 'single,' I always hesitated for a millisecond before I checked 'divorced.' It was at that moment that I allowed this formerly unconscious resentment to surface. All my life, I have refused to allow others to categorise me, yet it wasn't until then that I realised the degree to which I am categorised as a single woman. This workshop had raised my consciousness!

Choice or Circumstance

Another way that single women are often classified is whether we are single by choice or by circumstance. For me, it is a combination of each. I continue to have a desire to have a significant other in my life. So, in that sense, I don't choose to be single because I want to be. Rather, I have and continue to choose to be single because of the patriarchal nature of society and its notions of and expectations for marriage. For example, I am not willing to allow the government to decide if and when I can end a relationship. When I wanted to end my marriage, the only grounds for divorce were abuse, adultery, abandonment, or refusal to have conjugal relations. While none of these were the case, I had to claim that my spouse refused to have sex with me and even so, was only able to get a divorce because he did not contest it. Without legal grounds and my spouse's consent, I would not have been able to get out of a relationship that had become unbearable for me.

Since my divorce, freedom, independence, and space have become core needs and values for me. In terms of the traditional role of women in US society, my needs are outside the norm. At least in US society, women who express the need for freedom, independence, and space in relationships are perceived differently from men who do so. For men, these needs are considered the norm, while when women have them, we are seen as selfish, self-centred, stubborn, and headstrong. Even that terminology, to 'ask for' freedom, would never be used by men in the US. In fact, in US society, it is not unusual for men to have a room just for themselves: a 'study' or a 'den.' There is no equivalent for women to have a space for themselves unless it's for some traditional feminine activity such as sewing.

Wanting a relationship in which I can have freedom, independence, and space is difficult not simply because such a relationship is outside societal norms. It is also challenging because there are no models for creating relationships in which these needs can be met. In most cases, once married, or even partnered, patriarchal expectations come with the package.

Being single definitely comes with downsides. It can feel lonely and tiring to have to take care of everything on my own. Nevertheless, I prefer to cope with this reality than remain in any relationship that is less than nurturing and/or would leave me withered and unable to thrive.

Consequences

Being single for many years has left me stronger in many ways. I depend on myself for everything – ranging from financial support, home maintenance, and making major decisions, to caring for myself when I'm sick, and so forth. This strength, however, provides additional challenges to becoming partnered. It leaves me unconsciously denying my own vulnerability and often not able to ask for help. Also, some men are intimidated by my strength. Those who are attracted to me because of it are often unable to see my vulnerabilities. I do not doubt that their inability to see my vulnerabilities is a result of my having hidden them so well. In fact, they are often so deeply submerged that they are out of my own awareness as well.

Single Motherhood

More than being a single woman, I have been impacted by being a single mother. While I have been able to defy and live outside certain societal norms, the societal demands on mothers are ones I have not escaped. I, as much as society, pressured myself to play the role of mother to the highest standards – impossible standards, in fact. Anything less than being the perfect mother would mean I was a 'bad' mother – one of society's greatest crimes. I didn't put the same expectations for perfect parenting on my ex-husband. My having custody of both of our children did not make him any less of a good father. However, if the tables were turned and my ex-husband had custody of the children, and I saw them only every other weekend, I would be deemed villainous by society and myself. When women gain custody of their children after divorce, no negative assumptions are made about the fathers. On the other hand, when men gain custody, there is always an assumption that the mother was 'unfit' in some way. When a man's professional life leaves him with less time to spend with his children, that's taken as a given; when a woman's work takes time away from her children, there is no such automatic acceptance.

There are obvious challenges to being a single mother. What remains invisible to society, however, is the huge emotional toll it takes. I had to parent all the time. There was no partner to turn to when I needed a break or a time out. I couldn't ask anyone else to give the children a bath, tuck them in, dole out punishment, or simply give me some time alone. I had no backup when I got sick, or if work or an emergency came up that conflicted with my childcare responsibilities.

Being a parent is challenging under the best of circumstances; doing it alone without a partner to bounce ideas off, to help with decisions, or simply to tell me I'm doing a good job left me not only exhausted but often doubting myself. Despite having to play the role of both mother and father, I held myself to the same standards as a woman in a two-parent household and lived in fear of being seen as a failure if I was not able to be a superwoman and maintain those standards. Needless to say, I often felt like a failure.

Enjoying Being Single

Now that my children are grown and no longer live at home, I have become able to appreciate being on my own. While I would have loved to have someone to help me parent, without that need, I am happy being single. It makes it easier for me to create the life I want for myself. Rather than feeling deprived, I relish my freedom and independence. I enjoy and have embraced being single. If the right partner comes along, that would be lovely. But, I feel whole and complete whether that happens or not.

*****

My Life's Shades and Colours…

Archana Shrivastava, India

My Childhood Years

I was born in the state of Bihar in India. When I think of my childhood, certain memories stand out which have influenced my being single and the life I have created for myself as a single woman today.

Messages I got in my childhood that predominantly remained with me in my life for long years had themes like 'girls are…,' 'girls do…,' 'girls do not do…,' 'dowry is a must…,' 'boys are more…,' 'girls are less…,' 'studying in English medium is high status,' 'Hindi medium is below average,' and so on. My early life was filled with these messages and also trying to 'live up' to them for people close to me. I carried the burden of societal norms and values, which impacted my childhood, adolescence, and young adulthood in some very significant ways.

I felt less valued by others, especially by my parents and family members. In these circumstances, I also did not value myself for long years of my life. I grew up with feelings of:

Not being loved	Low confidence	High dependence on others
Not being valued	Low esteem	High trust on others
Not being good enough	Low self-image	High need to please others
Being less than...	Low trust in self	High pressure for performance

Quite early in my life, I started paying attention to the nuances of discriminatory societal norms and practices. I noticed how women are treated in our society, became aware and alarmed about the dowry system at the age of four (when a cousin sister was getting married), and gender discrimination at five or so (with my own experiences and observations). I experienced caste-based discrimination between five and six (when I was beaten up for eating at my friend's place, who was from a lower caste as per society) and witnessed the realities about how a widowed woman is treated in Hindu culture (when my maternal aunt became widow) when I was 15, and so on. I was clouded by the darkness of horrifying experiences from my childhood, mainly sexual abuse by my close and distant relatives, neighbours, and family friends, and those left deep scars on my mind, heart, and soul. It was more painful since I was left alone to deal with all such horrors. Whenever I tried talking to elders about it, I was discouraged from it and got no support from them. I learned to hide them as if it was my fault.

The way my elder brother and I got treated differently in the same house by my parents and other family members, and the sense of discrimination I experienced, became a significant contributor in shaping my adulthood. If the impact of that damage got reduced to some extent, it was because of a very sensitive person that I experienced in my brother. The backing and support that I found in him, in a way, encouraged me to ask questions and counter the values if they did not sit right within myself. A strong sense of the bond that I developed with him kept me going in life, collecting myself and reshaping me.

Ups and Downs in Academic Life (My Education)

A lot of experimentation happened with my education during my growing up. I surpassed all the barriers facing all situations. I was not sent for pre-school education, studied in a municipal corporation school with an informal environment (while my elder brother was sent to an English-medium missionary school), was forced to skip fifth standard, and was moved to a village school for a year in sixth standard since my mother was pursuing her graduation and was appearing for her final exams. As soon as my parents felt a little better financially, they moved me to an English-medium convent school, which was tough for me to cope with. I had an additional challenge in that I was compared with my brother every minute as he was studious. Reading was his passion and he was thus found with books most of the time. He performed well in his studies throughout. However, I appeared for the tenth and twelfth board examinations with my brother, even though he is two years older.

In spite of all the challenges, I survived because I guess I was a good student. I was not the studious kind but was pretty bright, as I used to rank first in the class, mostly, wherever I was studying. Tenth and twelfth were a bit extra challenging as I realised my foundation was weak and so I could not clear the competitive exams for medical entrance. I insisted, however, on taking up science as I was made to believe then that it is higher in status compared to pursuing arts or commerce. Irrespective of all challenges, I sailed through this period somehow. At the time of my twelfth board results, while all my family members were extremely happy, I remember crying because I had missed my first division by a few marks. It was painful and I felt small, as this had happened for the first time in my entire academic life.

After graduation, I wanted to undertake post-graduate studies to avoid early marriage and continue higher education, as I was enjoying my student life. My family values education, and thus was very supportive towards mine. When I entered a professional course, the Master's in Social Work at MS University, Vadodara, I found that

I had landed in the right place, where my interests, curiosity, and special capabilities in humanities could surface. I enjoyed my course and later took charge of my professional life, pursuing some diploma and certificate courses in psychology and counselling.

Grooming and Growing as a Girl

Like most Indian girls, I had continuously received a message that girls have to do everything right from a very young age towards preparation for their marriage. The way you talk, the way you laugh, looks, manners, behaviour, studies, household work, and so on. I suppose I fitted into the mould of expectations of a homely girl – the right material for marriage: softly spoken, well behaved, able to manage household work while good at academics and professional work too, someone who listened to elders, managed all boundaries, and valued relationships. At the same time, given what I was experiencing around me right from childhood, I wasn't sure if I wanted to get married at all. However, being the only daughter, my family had lots of dreams and expectations attached to my marriage. I thus believed that I had no option of not marrying, or of marrying someone of my choice.

I studied in girls' schools throughout my education. I guess it was considered safe to study in a girls' school. I wondered why the same thought was not there for the boy of the family, though. Till my graduation, I had minimal contact with boys. The only boys I knew or could interact with occasionally were my brother's friends. So, the only relationships I was allowed to make with boys outside my family were to tie 'Rakhi' (decorative threads that girls and women tie to their brothers) to them. I remember tying 'Rakhi' to some of my brother's friends. Probably they came over for the Rakhi festival, but actually they wanted to be friendly.

At the age of 21, during my post-graduate studies in social work, I had entered a co-ed college for the first time. Being a small batch, the entire class lived very closely with each other, almost like cousins. This was my first experience of direct interaction with the other gender. With camps and study tours being part of the curriculum, there were plenty of opportunities to interact with classmates. This created the issues and dilemmas for me, as I felt that I was almost committing a crime by talking to boys. I was busy maintaining as much distance as possible from my male classmates.

Search for a Marriage Partner

As I had come to believe that my parents have all the rights to decide who I will marry, I rejected some of the proposals that came my way during post-graduate study. My family started bringing some proposals as soon as I finished my post-graduate course. While I was ready to get in, I had by then developed some basic views about marriage:

- I wanted to marry without a dowry;
- I wanted to continue to work post marriage; and
- I also wanted my partner to respect me as a woman/person, and thus he must have an interest in who I am as a person.

All the proposals that came my way, unfortunately, did not fulfil these three basic criteria. Most stopped at the first stage itself, as dowry was an integral part of all the proposals. A girl aspiring to be a 'professional woman' was considered another irrational criterion at that point in time, at least in the families where proposals for me were in discussion. And with the third criterion, I think nobody (including my family members) understood what I wanted. Most proposals were blocked at the first and second criteria, and thus detailed discussion of the third never happened. Marriage remained a remote possibility as I could not find anyone who would consider my views. I was left wondering, "Was I expecting too much from marriage?" I don't think so... but the result was visible.

Around the age of 30, pressure and crisis at home for marriage, day in and day out, became very difficult to deal with. It was becoming unbearable to live with the situation with my family on a day-to-day basis. That's when I opted to move out of the city for professional work and build an independent life and identity. During this time, I became aware that while I had deep feelings for my parents, I was more closely bonded with my brother and had a strong dependence on him. I addressed my dependency, but continued a close relationship with him.

Living Away from Home

I moved out of my home and, for the first time, started living independently away from family members. While I remained closely connected with my brother and parents, I had some time and space to breathe independently. I continued to meet boys with a view to marriage as and when proposed by my family members. I made genuine efforts towards exploring the possibilities of finding a suitable partner.

On my own also, I did enter into some committed relationships with men and invested a lot in terms of a long span of my life and deep emotional engagements. My family had strong objections to inter-caste matches, but I fought the ground and remained committed to both my family as well as the relationships. I think I gave more than 100% to the relationships I was involved in and tried saving them to the best of my capacities. But relationships cannot be nurtured by one individual. They involve both partners committing to make it work. I was willing to give in and make many adjustments and compromises for them to survive and result in marriage. I hesitate to admit, however, that the men involved could not resist the objections and pressure from their families. They chose to go by what their family wanted them to do, and I don't really know to date what they wanted for themselves. I lost it – not once, but three times. Jokingly I say that "I had a few men in my life who loved me… but they did not love me enough."

As I understand it, my stand on dowry, caste, my professional identity, and the desire to seek respect from my partner kept coming in the way. Interestingly, there were hardly any conflicts in any of my relationships, yet they didn't materialise. I remember one of the men saying once that "You are too smart to be handled," which probably weakened him to take a stand. I also heard similar statements from some of the boys who came to see me for the purpose of marriage on previous occasions.

Gradually through this period, I was becoming a strong, confident woman with independent thinking on almost everything. I had ideas and opinions about the dowry system, the status of women and the respect they deserve, as well as women's travel, career growth, and support from home. And perhaps unknowingly, I sent out some messages which were scary for men to handle whilst remaining committed to the relationship. None of these relationships turned into a so-called recognised relationship in our society, one with the name of 'marriage.' The same story was also repeated when my family members seriously searched for a match for me through online marriage sites.

So I had never been closed to the idea of marriage – I wanted to marry, have my own family, child, and happiness, as it is commonly viewed in our society. However, I was never desperate; I did not want to marry just for the sake of marrying. My protest against dowry, my aspiration to establish a professional identity, and my independent thinking accompanied me throughout this period, ensuring that I remain unmarried and single.

Singlehood – An Opportunity for Development

As time passed, I accepted my single status, and that's when I started looking at alternate ways of living life, pursuing other dreams, and making efforts towards how else I wanted to enhance my life. A new stage of my life journey began, which was much more exploratory, curious, exciting, and eventful.

I grasped several opportunities to participate in development programmes using various applied behavioural science technologies, which became a major contributory factor in bringing many changes in my life. I entered ISABS (Indian Society for Applied Behavioural Science), and my journey of self-awareness and self-development began involving self-disclosure and engagement in deeper process work. I also sought professional support to work on my childhood experiences of sexual abuse, low self-image, addressing issues of rejection and pain, and so on. I built a new and refreshing relationship with 'self' and began to love myself almost for the first time. I embraced myself unconditionally, and that also helped me 'forgive' all the people who, as I saw, had caused so much pain and damage in my life.

I reframed my past by understanding the culture in which my parents grew up. My mother grew up in a family where the girl had to do all the work for everyone in the house (including four brothers), even while studying like her brothers. She also grew up with some values – 'boys are…' and 'girls are…' – in a large family which understood over-protectiveness as 'extra love' for girls. My father lost both his parents very early in his childhood. His sisters were married off early, and he lived like an orphan, largely dependent on his close and distant relatives like his maternal and paternal uncles. He served all of them day and night, endlessly. In turn, he had a roof over his head and also some elders around. He had almost no voice of his own to express his opinions. After her marriage (at 18), my mother was greatly dependent on my father's uncles and aunts for all the decisions of their life. There was a culture of obeying elders blindly without any questioning, any complaint, dialogue on any current challenges, or disagreements. My mother had a hard time cooking meals three times a day and serving a large family of more than 35 people, including dogs. Seeing this context, I am now appreciative of my parents' resilience and efforts in the way they finally brought up me and my brother. They had all their dreams around their children and lived a very hard life to achieve them.

Hence, I came to accept that much of my suffering and pain from my childhood experiences of discrimination and stress was not caused purposely by anyone. It was much more rooted in their upbringing and the deep messages they had received on social norms in their growing stage. However, I do feel that it should have been of crucial importance for my family and society to ensure that I had a childhood free from exploitation, fear, and pain.

Once I healed myself and moved ahead into the present, leaving my past sufferings behind, I had a new perspective on life. I rebuilt my relationship with my parents afresh; I started seeing episodes from my past from other dimensions as well: the black and dark colours started showing some shades of whites and grey, and some pink, blue, and orange started popping out. I kind of released myself from bondages. I remember saying at one point that I didn't seem to remember any pleasant events from childhood and thus didn't feel like travelling those memory lanes ever. Now when I look back, there are many things from that same childhood which bring back joy and put a smile on my face.

A positive approach to living life and deriving satisfaction from work helped me channel my anger and negative energy towards helping other individuals and groups in need. This, in turn, also helped in mending myself with love and care and become much stronger than before. I made a movement towards:

- Loving self
- Valuing self
- Accepting self
- Being content and happy with whoever I am – and not comparing myself with others
- More self-confidence
- Building self-esteem
- Constructing a positive self-image
- Trusting self and others
- Independence
- Focusing on my own needs and values rather than pleasing others
- Pushing my boundaries and performing
- And finally, self-worth…

On the professional front, being single has been advantageous in building my career in many ways, as I have been continuously engaged in upgrading my professional skills and competencies. I am living the value of 'learning' to a great extent. I have had the freedom and time to work, as I had no major family responsibilities for long years of my life. I could commit myself fully without many restrictions. I have been open to travel extensively for work, have used most of the opportunities available, and was always ready to take on any new challenges that were offered or created.

However, sometimes as a professional, even now, I do experience a sense of discrimination compared to my male counterparts. Being single sometimes exposes me to unnecessary doubts and exclusion. I have noticed that some of my male friends who are also professional colleagues maintain a distance from me, mainly because I am not married. I don't get invited to events by them, even professional gatherings, I guess, because their spouses might feel threatened.

Life as a Single Mother

One significant part of my identity today is 'single mother.' I dreamt of marriage, a partner, a family of a certain kind, and most of it did not happen. I modified the dream and made a family of my own differently by adopting a girl child into my life. She completed me as a woman, mother, and person. Because of her, I think I have better access and acceptance in my family and society, and also a more complete life. As I write here, I see that this has filled my life with a range of emotions – pride, joy, challenges, pain, sorrow, burden, self-doubt, responsibility, opportunity, social acceptance, as well as rejection.

This is one *big dream* in my life that got fulfilled, and probably the *only* one. I felt so happy and blessed that I could make it happen, and then my lovely daughter held my hand and walked into my life with her tiny and soft feet. This experience of mine says that I have not had anything in my life that came easily to me; bringing up a child is also challenging, but at least it happened.

Society's response is kind of extreme sometimes. As I experience it, society, on the whole, does not approve or respect single status. At the same time, many married women are envious or jealous of me, perhaps because of my visible freedom, independence, and happiness. They are not able to see my invisible responsibilities, challenges, struggles, and roadblocks. A few are appreciative, and I receive unconditional love and acceptance from those special people.

Seeing me as a single adoptive mother, many feel and express that I am like a 'real superwoman,' and they put me on a pedestal for this decision of mine, for supporting a life, doing good to someone. They appreciate me for being courageous, brave, a huge risk-taker, strong, and so on. Sure, I am all that, but I also know that I am doing this for my own needs. I am very well aware that I brought this girl into life for a reason that is pretty different from those imagined or believed by many in society. My situation was that I badly wanted my baby; I badly wanted to fulfil my personal need of loving my baby, being loved by her, being deeply connected with another person in my life. I am thankful to her for bringing love and intimacy into my life. That actually humbled me to a great extent, and at no point in time was there an expectation of any return from her. I value and relish the love, care, respect, and recognition that I received and continue to receive from her. I chose to provide my daughter with a family and not only a mother. Thus, I moved back to live with my parents to seek their support in raising her. I enrolled her in the same school where her cousins (my brother's kids) were studying, to avoid some amount of discrimination within the family. We have been living in the mainstream of society where we are together dealing with challenges. I started to work as a consultant, leaving my job to have the flexibility and strike a balance between availability as a mother and my professional engagements. I have provided her a range of examples and experiences of families and parenting, and exposed her to various activities – sports, music, dance, school, drawing, acting, social spaces, and so on. Besides this, I have also planned holidays, fun, and celebrations with her. We have also built a support group of like-minded people – a single adoptive mothers' group. I believe I have put in efforts to bring different colours into her life, and I feel happy and proud as a mother. However, it has been (and continues to be) a challenge to create enough financial resources to support her in her studies and growth, now and into the future.

My daughter is in her teens now, and we are both in this critical phase of life, full of changes and challenges like most other teens and their mothers/parents. Various things about her that affect me today and put me in the category of 'worried mother' include her academic performance, attitude and behaviour, her ways of dealing with things, her growth and development, her addiction to gadgets and material things, and most importantly her safety. I feel the need to protect her from being hurt as much as possible.

I think I have been performing my responsibilities as I see right at all stages. However, I go through my own sets of dilemmas – Is it right for her? Am I contributing enough to shape her life positively? What am I worried about and why – my failure or her losses and future, or both? What do I want her to be – good in society or a happy person? And what is she becoming actually? I believe it is fair to raise these questions, find my answers from within and around, and act as feels right at the moment. I guess parenting in all situations is challenging, but probably there are added factors here: that my daughter is adopted, she is being raised without a father, and maybe because she is a girl. It is an extra struggle sometimes to play all the roles by myself, and I do miss having a companion to share the process and the impact of decision making. However, I am aware that many women do this despite the fathers being alive or around or otherwise. So, my single-mother identity brings all that stuff which brings joy and happiness as well as challenges, pushing me to raise my bar and to exercise creativity, innovation, and perseverance.

When I speak of challenges or sometimes when I seek support, the messages I get back predominantly are "Who asked you to get into this mess?" or "You are responsible for the mess." This is quite painful for me. If the same child had been born biologically and within wedlock, no one would make such comments or inferences. But just because this is not linked with marriage and the natural biological birth of the child, and I am a single woman choosing motherhood by adopting a child, my daughter and I are exposed to such comments.

My family and close friendship circle are generally supportive, and we all have learnt and grown together with my life of singlehood and being a single adoptive mother of a daughter. I have a support system to fall back on, and I have helping hands to raise her. Besides, I also care about my needs, looking after myself, keeping myself happy, doing work that satisfies me, shopping to please myself, indulging in happy and meaningful friendships, openly sharing and seeking spaces and opportunities to nurture myself. My work provides me opportunities to recharge myself when I am away from home. I am able to see things from different perspectives and come back better equipped to handle the situation and challenges.

My Critical Challenges

Initially, I came back home after adopting my daughter to seek support from my parents in raising her. Later, when my parents were ageing, they needed support. My being single has made it obvious and convenient for all of us that I take up a caring role for them. My father is now no more, and my mother lives with me. I do receive support from my mother in many ways. However, more often, my role as giver becomes heavier than as receiver, and that creates pressure and imbalance. Life these days is balancing between my daughter, me, and my mother, with wide gaps of age amongst the three. I oscillate between being strong and being vulnerable with the expression of anger and pain, considering its impact on my daughter. I am not getting satisfactory results in the role of disciplining and boundary setting for my daughter. It is challenging to take decisions for both my mother and daughter without having a sounding board. I feel the need to take a pause and nurture myself before I continue to be in giving roles. I have also realised strongly that I have to be the primary caretaker for myself as well.

Being single also means that I have to fall back on people other than family at times for support. This identity has consequences. I feel independent; people perceive me as independent, and sometimes even when in need, I am very hesitant and careful in asking for help. I tend to be more in a giving mode than a receiving one, and at the same time, I also find myself reacting when more is expected out of me.

Who I Have Become Today

I believe I play all my roles in personal and professional space pretty well, not excelling in any but nowhere near failing either. I feel proud that I took the courage to ask questions or rock the boat every time something did not fit my values and needs. At the same time, I also utilised my patience and perseverance to allow my family and other people in my life to accept the change and grow. As a result, I still feel supported by them, and I continue to support them. Despite all the challenges, I feel good that my daughter and I are integrated into our family and society to a great extent. Being open and authentic in sharing comfortably about my status and identity as a *single woman* in all spaces, including the home front, workspaces, my daughter's school, and friendship circle, has reduced the burden of hiding facts and living under pressure. I feel good about myself, having lived around half of my life on my own terms. I carved my path by reshaping values and beliefs, and also balancing and following other social norms.

*****

In Pursuit of Learning and Freedom

Vidya Gupta, India[1]

To me, being single means having the freedom to learn, explore, and develop my full potential. It means being able to expand my horizons beyond traditional roles and the little corner of the earth I was born in. It means being able to pursue my interests and passions, travel, meet people, and immerse myself in different cultures. It also means enjoying almost all aspects of family and social life. It means living life to the fullest, without any regrets!

All-round Development Fostered in Childhood

I remember my childhood as being quite ideal. I was the youngest of three siblings, and we grew up in a gated community with ample space to play and lots of children of the same age to play with. After returning from school, we would rush outside to play with our friends for a good two hours. We played such a wide variety of traditional games, climbed trees, and really enjoyed the outdoor playground equipment such as swings, parallel bars, seesaws, and the jungle gym. We also participated in various community activities,

---

1 This is a pseudonym.

including celebrating the various Indian festivals like Holi, Navratri, Diwali, and watching films, staging plays, dances, and so forth.

I went to an all-girls school, where we were encouraged to take leadership and participate in a variety of activities. I remember being nominated as one of the four class captains all through my school years. Also, I played sports, participated in the annual-day dance performances, the march pasts on Republic Day, and the school fairs to raise funds for charity. I was good at my studies and was quite popular with some teachers, especially during my primary education. At home too, my parents were invested in our all-round development and took the initiative to enrol me for training in classical dance, sports, and drawing. They encouraged us to read books. I remember that while we had a limited budget to spend on clothes, my father gave us free rein on purchasing as many books as we wanted. We had access to several newspapers, periodicals, comics, and libraries. He also indulged us with a lot of informal learning and exposure by taking us with him on his fieldwork in the districts (he was a government official), where he would arrange for us to visit and understand the intricate workings of dams, windmills, mines, factories, farms, and suchlike. I remember my father initiating discussions at the dinner table on current issues and diverse topics and purposefully playing devil's advocate to instigate debate and prompt us to defend our stands. On reflection, the wonderful opportunities of formal and informal education, and all-round development that my parents provided me within my childhood have contributed significantly to mould me into a strong, confident, and well-rounded person.

I also imbibed many of the values that I treasure from my parents, viz. hard work, integrity, and compassion. My father was extremely sincere towards his work and often brought it home, many a time working late into the night. My grandpa would sometimes find him asleep at his desk late at night and wake him up and ask him to go to bed. He was also incorruptible as a government official, and we hear stories of his integrity from total strangers to this day. Such integrity cost him in terms of multiple and frequent transfers from one department to another in the government. But he stayed true to his values right till the end of his tenure. My mother, too, worked very hard, looking after the home and us – three children, my grandpa, and my father. I remember her picking us up from school to take us directly to dancing class and thoughtfully packing and bringing along our dress change, snacks, and drinks. She would also take us to the club for swimming lessons, despite her busy schedule. Besides this, she also took care of several troubled persons from our extended family, who sought refuge in our home from time to time. Consequently, she taught us about caring and compassion through her own example in life.

Love for Learning

From the stories narrated by my parents, I was a child eager to learn. As I was the youngest of three children, I wanted to follow my sister and brother to school. Every day, I would pack a little bag and ask my grandpa to take me to school. He would have to take me out of the house and show me a closed house or shop to convince me that my school was closed, and then bring me back home. This happened so many times that soon, my grandpa got tired of it and asked my mother to enrol me in a school. She spoke to the principal of my brother's school and was told that I was too young to start school. Even then, my mother persisted and requested the principal to just meet me once before deciding. The principal met me and asked me a bunch of questions, which I was able to answer satisfactorily, much to the principal's surprise. And so, I was admitted to school at a very young age. On the first day of school, when most children cry when their parents leave, my mother said that I did not even look back to bid her goodbye, and when she returned to collect me at the end of the school day, I wanted to remain in school and not return home. Another story is about how I stubbornly refused to miss school when my parents had to travel, and they had to arrange for me to stay with family friends so that I could attend. One threat that always worked on me was that if I didn't do a certain thing, I would not be allowed to attend school the next day. So, my love for learning and the priority that I assigned to it started very young and have sustained through the years.

Search for My Interests and Passion

My educational and work journey has involved a number of changes and experimentation for finding and living my passion. I shifted from the science stream in the tenth standard to the commerce stream for my higher secondary education, as I discovered that the former was not a good fit for me, though I performed well. During my undergraduate studies, I realised that my interest was oriented towards human resources and that my interest in computer science was because I enjoyed solving logical challenges and was good at it. However, I was disillusioned with the education system as it was not challenging enough. So instead of pursuing post-graduate studies, which was the norm, I was eager to enter the real world of work.

I did a diploma in computer programming and applications and then joined as a faculty member. For the next seven years, I taught computer science to various age groups, experimented with different job profiles – from faculty to marketing executive to centre manager – and found that I was good at teaching and personnel management and development. I enrolled as an external student with the state university, studied independently, and completed my post-graduate studies in commerce to join a premier national-level management institute as an academic associate and assisted with the teaching. While I enjoyed my work there, I was interested in developing myself further but did not get the further development opportunity in that job. As someone who was always on a quest for new knowledge and exploring my abilities, I decided to change tracks once again.

It took a long phase of experimentation and discovery to find my real interests. I believe that this was possible due to my being single. I could focus on understanding and developing myself as a person.

Radical Views about Marriage and Family

I remember being against the idea of an arranged marriage when I was young. I could not fathom how anyone could get to know another person well enough to decide to spend a lifetime together within the span of a few meetings. Also, I remember asking if I was a vegetable or something that a boy would come to see me. I did not think that I should get married just because I was of a certain age. Also, pursuing work of my choice and interest was a top priority in my life, and I was not ready to compromise on that front. The traditional role of women in our society never really appealed to me. I remember arguing with my father when I was quite young about why I was expected to help my mother in the kitchen while my brother was not. I was more interested in running errands outside the house, which were assigned to my brother. Even today, I have no interest in cooking and housekeeping and only see them as subsistence tasks. However, I thought that I should act like a good daughter to my parents and give arranged marriage a shot. But when the very first boy came to see me, I felt so uncomfortable with the entire process that I told my parents that, since I would be unhappy in such a marriage, how could my partner and my and his parents be happy? So, it didn't make sense if it was not going to make anyone happy. Thankfully, my parents were agreeable and decided not to go ahead with it.

I was and am open to love, but I never actively searched for a partner on my own either. I attribute that to always feeling whole as a person and never feeling incomplete. I never felt anything to be missing, and therefore never felt the need to look for a partner. I assumed that if I met someone I really liked, I could always take time to get to know him, fall in love, and get married at any time in my life. Also, I am a person with some radical thoughts regarding marriage and family. I expect a marriage to be a relatively well-balanced relationship between a mature man and woman, with each pulling his or her weight and working together to make it a success. The roles within such a marriage should be worked out as per the individuals' respective skills and preferences, not as per tradition. The purpose should be that both the partners enjoy working together to achieve their potentials and raise good human beings. Also, you don't necessarily have to create these human beings, as there are already many out there who have either been abandoned or orphaned, and you can very well love them and provide them with a home and family. I knew that my radical thoughts on these issues were, and still are, a difficult proposition in our culture and society. I am yet to meet someone who views marriage in the same light.

Singlehood and Professional Adventures

Being single became an opportunity to keep searching and experiment with various work profiles and find a meaningful profession. I had been interested in public services since my father was a government official. However, he had advised me against opting for it, as he found, from his own experience, that there was very little scope for an honest officer to do good work within a system that was increasingly plagued with corruption. I always wondered about what it would be to work from outside the system to try and fix it. Consequently, to explore the field of development, I found a position with a non-governmental organisation (NGO) and worked with them in the villages of Rajasthan for the next six years, experimenting with different job profiles. It was a very adventurous, enlightening, and satisfying time for an urban, middle-class girl like me, who was not much acquainted with the realities of the rural poor in India. I felt that I had finally found my calling. But after observing that there was minimal knowledge capture and sharing amongst the NGOs, resulting in everyone wasting time and resources in reinventing the wheel, I thought that I could contribute more to this field by developing myself further as a researcher. So, I took up a position as a development expert on a community health pilot project. During this time, I also sent applications to study abroad, as I was unconvinced of the quality of doctoral studies in India.

I was awarded a scholarship to attend a prestigious university in the United States for a doctoral programme in human resource development. I lived and worked there assisting teaching and research for five years. It was a wonderful learning experience, not only due to my programme but also from being immersed in a different country and culture. Being located in Washington, DC gave me the opportunity to attend seminars, conferences, and the like at world-class institutions and by various heads of nations and ambassadors. After completing my coursework, I returned home to take care of my parents, who were ageing and suffering from some serious health ailments, and worked on my doctoral dissertation while doing this. This was another gift of being single, that I could be a support to my parents when needed.

Single but Not Alone

So, was I really single, except in the sense of not being married? Yes, I am unmarried and therefore 'single,' but I have never really lived alone. Almost all my life, I have lived with my parents. For a relatively short span of five years, when I lived abroad and away from my parents, the financial constraints of being an international student dictated that I live with roommates. That was itself a very enriching experience, as I got to live with girls from around the world, which expanded my worldview further. As I have lived as a part of a family, I have never felt alone as a single woman. My parents, siblings, aunts, uncles, cousins, and their spouses have always been an important part of my life. I got to love and closely associate with children from birth to adulthood, especially with my two nieces and, to some extent, with my cousins' children too. Also, I make friends easily and have a lot of friends from school, college, university, and all the places I have worked in to share with and keep me company. I love and enjoy my work and spend most of my time focused on it. It involves a lot of interaction with people. I also love to read, watch movies, listen to music, enjoy the performing arts, attend exhibitions of art, crafts, and design, listen to lectures and seminars on diverse topics, travel, be with nature, do photography, and more. And I will do all these things by myself, as I do not always need company. In fact, I enjoy time alone and sometimes even need it.

Challenges as a Single Woman

I have faced some challenges as a single woman, mostly to do with a mindset greatly influenced by patriarchy. The first incident that comes to my mind is what the state governor said to me at my sister's wedding reception. I had just completed my bachelor's degree and was excited about joining the workforce or pursuing higher education. He said that now that my sister was married, it had cleared my line to get married too! I was quite shocked that a person holding such a high public office had only this to say to someone poised at the beginning of her career. I was quite angry with him for his stereotypical remark and expectation. Unfortunately, this same pattern was followed by relatives, strangers, and sometimes even extended family for the next 10–15 years of my life. Initially, as I was young, my reaction would be one of anger or annoyance, and I would argue with them about how their stereotypical expectations did not fit in with my aspirations. However, as I grew older and more experienced, I learned to take these remarks and questions in my stride and respond at first with jest and later even attempted to educate them. Even when I was leaving for my education abroad, a couple of men from my family surprised me with their conventional thinking as they tried to dissuade me from taking that step. Thankfully, I was quite resolute and confident in pursuing my goals and was not deterred by the advice of such mindsets.

Another challenge I faced was from some supervisors and colleagues who had some strange assumptions about single women. They thought that since I was not married, I did not have any responsibilities at home and could be called upon to work overtime on weekdays and weekends. Why would I not have any responsibilities at home? Did I not live with a family, just like them? And doesn't every member of the family have certain responsibilities towards the home and the family? And even if I lived alone, did I not have the right to leisure on the weekend? These were the questions that came to my mind, and I expressed them quite clearly and openly to my supervisors and colleagues. I did not allow myself to be exploited by their unfair, ill-founded, and unrealistic assumptions and expectations.

My Support System

My parents have been the biggest supporters of my life journey. They have supported me in every possible way. The first and most important support that I received from them is their unconditional love. That has been the main reason why I have felt so confident and secure all my life. I have met enough other people who did not receive such unconditional love from their parents and were scarred for life. The other support that my parents gave me, which I greatly value, is understanding and accepting my choice to be single. I am sure that they faced flak from society for this, but they never ever pressure me to conform, and I am thankful to them for that. Yes, they were hopeful that I would meet and marry someone at some point in life, but they never forced me to marry. And last but certainly not least, it was their financial support that was extremely helpful because it allowed me to explore my interests, pursue my education, and discover myself and my passion in life. Without this invaluable support, I would not have been able to do everything that I wanted to and could do in my life. In adulthood, my sister has been my greatest cheerleader and pillar of strength. We share a relationship which is rare even amongst siblings. We are very different personalities, but we totally understand and immensely love and respect each other. In good times and bad times, she is always there for me, and I know for sure that she will always be there for me and vice versa.

There was no precedent of single unmarried women in my family before me. I am the first one to walk this path. I have probably become an inspiration for a few others in the family. However, I have a lot of friends who either chose or ended up being single. Those who selected to be single mostly did so because they had clearly outlined goals and wanted to live life on their own terms, while others wanted to get married but did not find the right partner and were not desperate enough to settle for just about anyone. Most of these friends are living wholesome and healthy lives. However, a few of them are emotionally insecure and sometimes quite depressed. These are the ones who wanted to get married but did not find a suitable partner. Those who live away from their families sometimes feel guilty about not being able to look after their ageing or ailing parents. They sometimes have to deal with neighbours who assume that, as they live alone, they are probably lonely and therefore try to give them company even when they want to be left alone to relax.

Thoughts on Marriage and Society

I observe that amongst my married friends, some are in happy and well-balanced marriages with supportive in-laws. Some got married only because they were insecure and lacked the confidence to live alone. Some stay in unhappy marriages for the sake of children or to avoid the social stigma of divorce, or due to financial dependence and being used to a standard of life they think they cannot sustain by themselves. Most suppress or compromise on their aspirations and live their entire life in the service of their families. That is probably why many of them tell me that I made a good choice in staying single and are often envious of my life.

I understand that marriage and family are structures designed by society to ensure some order, especially after human beings started settling down in one place and had to organise to live together in large numbers. However, I would like society to evolve to be able to respect some divergence from the norm. People who choose to live outside the accepted societal structures should be able to live normal and full lives without being subject to unnecessary scrutiny and suspicion. I also believe that the patriarchal design of these structures needs to change to accommodate the worldview of the other 50% of society. If this does not happen, these structures will gradually become strained, create conflict, and their very purpose will be lost.

Ready for Change

As I was completing my dissertation research, my father passed away. After completing and being awarded my doctorate, I started working on a part-time basis as a visiting professor while still looking after my mother. Recently, I lost my mother too. I am now looking for a full-time position in academia with my research focused on studying learning, leadership, and change related to the sustainable development of rural communities.

My life is currently poised for a major change as I have lost both my parents, and I need to get ready to live by myself. As I search for a full-time position in a good organisation, it could take me outside my hometown and possibly even out of the country. This would mean being at a distance from my family and friends, who are an important part of my support system. However, this does not scare me in any way. Instead, I find myself excited to face the new adventures and experiences that await me.

I look forward to discovering the new organisation that I will become a part of and learning the reins of my new work, creating a new home, and making new friends and relationships. As Eleanor Roosevelt beautifully articulated, "The purpose of life is to live it, to taste experience to the utmost, to reach out eagerly and without fear for newer and richer experience."

*****

An Unexpected and (Mostly) Happy State of Being

Sharon L. Miller, USA

It was with some surprise that I found myself single at the age of 50. It shouldn't have been a surprise – for I had, in fact, never seriously dated anyone, so obviously had not married either. I realised though that most of my friends were married or in long-term committed relationships or had recently left a marriage/partnership. I had not. And I was happy.

I had never made a specific decision to remain single, but here I was. Perhaps because I was raised by a strong single mother, I never saw singleness as a handicap. Perhaps because I was not exposed to a loving marriage relationship in my childhood, I never longed for the companionship of marriage. Perhaps because my mother never let her single state keep her from doing precisely what she wanted to do, I never thought I needed a husband to be complete. Perhaps because I identify as lesbian, I never dated men, much less married one. Perhaps because our society (and certainly my family) does not encourage or affirm same-sex relationships, I remained single.

Perhaps.

It's just as likely that I had simply gotten on with my life.

Other people seem to have had a harder time with my singleness than I did. The assumption seems to be that if a woman is single, and has never married, there has to be some obvious or hidden flaw that has kept her from being chosen as a bride. Since I am reasonably attractive and intelligent, and play well with others, I have had friends and near-strangers puzzle over my singleness. Perhaps I had an unfortunate love affair? No. Perhaps I am afraid of men? No. Perhaps I am afraid of commitments? No.

The underlying premise is that we all should be coupled; we all should have a mate, a husband or wife. To not have one is somehow going against the natural order of life. I would like to believe that the concern others have shown over my singleness springs from the fact that they have found great love and happiness in a significant relationship, and they wish the same for me. But I also wonder if there is some unacknowledged envy. I am a free, autonomous spirit in their eyes. I seek no one's permission for the life I lead. I need not compromise my life's ambitions or my choices for dinner. I set my own schedule, make my own rules, and determine my own bedtime.

It's true, there is much to be envied in the single life, and I have no regrets. I am 66 now and can look back with pride on my travels and adventures, the degrees I worked hard to earn and my career in academia. It has been a good life, a rich life, and I am grateful beyond words.

I have not been independent though; I did not get here by myself. Singleness has given me the freedom to develop a deep and broad network of friends that spans the world. I have a great capacity for love and, because it is not channelled towards a primary relationship, I am available to others. I have learned to give and receive, to sacrifice for others, and ask for help. My friendships have made me the whole person that I am today, for they have taught me love and intimacy in vulnerability. If I had not learned these lessons, I would be a solitary, lonely being.

There are downsides to being single, and these include when help is needed, having none immediately at hand – the flat tire on the highway, being desperately sick in the middle of the night, or the very large spider in the bathroom – or times when I wish for a companion to share a moment of adventure or delight like a stunning view of the mountains or a trek in Nepal.

But there has also been a dark side to being single, and that is the fear I live with because of my vulnerability as a woman. I don't remember a time when I wasn't afraid, for every day, there are news reports of women being assaulted, raped, or killed. I am not by nature a hysterical person, nor one given to exaggeration or alarm. And yet I know, in my bones I know, that what has befallen other women could happen to me simply because I am female. I have had first-hand experience of the danger. I have heard the catcalls and kissing noises, seen the suggestive hand signals and leering smirks, and dodged the groping hands (sometimes unsuccessfully), and have been assaulted.

I want to assert, in my defence, that I have always dressed and behaved modestly and am not a person of great beauty – as if those claims should somehow protect me from these unwanted advances and assaults. The fact is, it hardly matters what I wear or how I look; being female in our society and culture is enough to garner unwanted attention. And to be a single female doubles the danger, anxiety, and fear.

I wonder how many women get married in part because it's the safest thing to do. In many traditions, a woman remains under the protection and authority of her father until she is transferred to the protection and authority of her husband. To be without this protection is dangerous – as any single woman can tell you. When a woman is with a man in the street or marketplace – whether he be father, husband, or even brother – she can be assured that the catcalls will not come and the groping hands will not reach for her breasts. Men, who themselves may be guilty of harassment, are all too willing to step up to the role of protector. They are conditioned for this – to protect what is theirs, to guard against any violation of 'their property.'

When I was a young adult and travelling in Bangladesh, I had to catch a flight from Cox's Bazar to Dhaka. I was driven to the airport by a male family friend, who scanned the airport waiting room when we arrived. Upon spotting an older gentleman, travelling with what appeared to be his wife and children, 'George' made a bee-line to him and introduced me. Would he (the stranger) be so kind as to see that I safely arrived in Dhaka and met my friends at the airport? "Of course," the gentleman agreed. I sat down demurely next to his wife, waiting for our flight. I had been successfully 'handed off' to another male, and all was well in the world. Even a male stranger can, if need be, step into the role of protector for a lone woman.

It is true that when a woman walks down the street or goes to market, whether she is married or single, catcalls and suggestive remarks and danger may follow her if she is alone. But to be young (or not so young), single, and female is to be vulnerable to attacks in a way that most married women are not.

I ask myself, what would I have done in life as a single woman if I had not been afraid? I would have travelled unafraid. I have travelled alone many times, but rarely unafraid. I would have walked alone under the night sky. I would have hiked the Appalachian Trail. I would have visited countries I dared not visit as a single woman. I would have taken the subway home late at night by myself, rather than pay for a taxi. I would set out on adventures without feeling the pit in the bottom of my stomach, the small anxious voice that wonders if I'll be safe.

The biggest problem I've faced as a single woman has not been that I don't have a spouse or partner; it has been my vulnerability as a single woman. This is not a problem of my marital status; this is a problem of patriarchy, which objectifies women and assumes that single women are fair game. I had long assumed that I would no longer be afraid when I was old or older and had white hair. I have white hair, I'm in my sixth decade, and I'm still afraid.

Singleness is a choice for some; for others (including me), circumstances and life's path have led to this state. I don't for a moment regret my single state – I only wish the fear would leave me.

*****

The Tortoise on the Road

Rita Aggarwal, India

The Road Less Travelled

> Two roads diverged in a wood, and I –
> I took the one less traveled by,
> And that has made all the difference.
>
> Robert Frost[1]

It's tough to tell my story with an honesty and openness that are not embarrassing in some parts. In short, the road of singlehood has been rough on the personal as well as professional front. Today, at the age of 65, as I look back, I realise it has been a long journey. The undulating road offered unique experiences with risks, potholes, and adventure, but a satisfying one at this point. I have no regrets about the way I have navigated it. The choices I made at various stages were the best I could at that time. I habitually churned my mind about the good and bad choices I made and took ownership of all that happened. Nobody else was responsible. As a principle, I wanted to conduct my life and behaviour with grace and dignity.

---

1 Robert Frost, 'The Road Not Taken,' Retrieved 20 November 2022. Source: https://www.poetryfoundation.org/poems/44272/the-road-not-taken

My experiences made me wiser, mature, and taught me to refine my thoughts, emotions, and attitudes towards life. Singlehood taught me many lessons. Long hours of solitude helped cultivate the virtues of patience, reticence, and resilience. I learnt to master my emotions, transcend my desires and unrealistic expectations, and devote myself to duty and work. I evolved myself into a good human being and grounded myself in reality, embracing my limitations. Today I take care of my parents as my duty and love for them. I feel obliged with a deep sense of gratitude for their unconditional love and support.

After struggling without role models at home to inspire me for a career and no lamp-posts to guide me on my path of education, I was happy to have arrived in 1992 as the first psychologist in Central India in private practice. It was undoubtedly destiny that created a larger design and purpose for me. If success is judged by the value you create for the benefit of society and the ethical values you stand for with confidence and conviction, then I am a successful woman. I am happy with my professional accomplishments as well as my personal sanity, which I find to be far superior to those of many of my married contemporaries! I have attained this state with hard work, dedication, discipline, and sacrifice.

Good Beginnings

I was born in the coalfields of Jharkhand, North India. It was a self-contained industrialised township away from the city. As a child, I was anxious, shy, and submissive. Who am I? What is the purpose of my life? Why was I born? These were questions that always played in my mind like a background score, as far as I can remember. My siblings and friends did not seem to be bothered with philosophical speculations as I was. They seemed so confident and sure of themselves.

My parents were tradition-bound and strict disciplinarians, and we obediently followed the rules. We were encouraged to achieve in school in all ways. I seemed to have inherited or imbibed that. I remember having an intense desire to beat a specific classmate of mine at the flat race in school, and I did. She had been one tough competitor. I had been trying to achieve the number one position on the victory stand for a year, and I finally did it. It was an athletic challenge I set up for myself at middle school as I was no good at team games, being extremely shy, and not interested in being with other people. It was the same with academics – I had to excel and be ahead of others. I was not aggressively competitive but always liked to push myself forward. I was never a backbencher. Some classmates called me a boring bookworm. Others called me a snob. I felt misunderstood by them and was unable to communicate my true feelings. Being shy and introverted, I did have a problem expressing myself. At most times, I would hide them and suppress them.

Since education was a priority for my parents, they sent us to the best elite convent schools in the region. Because these were far from our home, we were in the hostel from nursery, which was hard on me, I remember. But hostel life in the convent imbued me with a disciplined routine, good behaviour, and good habits. I developed a strong sense of fairness and justice, which landed me in trouble many times.

Being a Girl

As children, our parents treated the three of us the same. This changed, however, when it came to matters of marriage and career. My brother, who was younger than me, was groomed by my father to take up engineering like himself; my career plans were never discussed. I was allowed to study and make my own choices, but I was often told that marriage was the ultimate career for girls, according to societal dictates.

What it means to be a 'girl' in society started dawning on me when my parents started talking about getting my elder sister married while she was still in the tenth standard (I was in the eighth standard then). My sister, who had dreams of becoming a medical doctor, was disturbed by these discussions of marriage. The process of finding a match for her was a painful one: the hunting for a groom, demands of dowry, visits of interested families, and the fuss my parents created were annoying and distasteful. I had decided that this type of marriage was not for me, and I would not allow myself to be bullied by anyone. I did not like domination and did not fit into the socialised role of a 'good' daughter-in-law or wife. Being single seemed to be the right choice for me as I got exposed to the various demands of traditional marriage. Hearing the stories of unhappy married women, I began to form a view that if the choice is between being miserable in marriage and being miserable alone, I would choose the second option. As I stood on the threshold of adulthood, I was beginning to think seriously about making a career instead of marriage, but I was quite confused and could not think of who would help me with guidance and planning.

A Life-defining Condition: A Millstone around My Neck

During my early teens, I was diagnosed with a lung condition, chronic obstructive lung disease (COPD), which they said was a common ailment in the coal-mines where I was brought up. The disease restricted all outdoor physical activities – but initially, my spirit refused to accept my limitations. Although my body was constrained, my mind could be free with great fantasy and hope. My intelligence in academics was a boon for me, and I began to cultivate indoor interests such as reading, writing, watching movies, and indoor games. Painfully, however, I started understanding and accepting my limitations as the disease took priority over everything. I could no longer take my health for granted – I had to care for it on a daily basis. My father prepared me by stating "Life is a struggle for all – for you, it will be a double struggle."

It became progressively clearer to me that marriage and motherhood would be too tough for me with my quiet nature and fragile health. A typical marriage primarily demands the woman to be a good wife, a good homemaker, a good daughter-in-law, and a mother of children. Her career and intelligence are secondary or redundant. I did not seem to qualify for it. Better to live alone and make some meaning of my life, I thought. I had many offers of marriage, as I was an attractive young lady with intelligence and good looks, but I shunned them all. Others thought I was a snob and a proud female.

When it was my turn for matchmaking, I informed my parents, somewhat sternly, not to subject me to harassment for marriage like my sister. "I would stand on my own feet," I said to them. Being single was a certainty unless I found someone who was like-minded and liked me too. I was preparing myself for a road less travelled.

Voices of Different Women

During the mid-1970s I was at the University of Ranchi, Jharkhand, in North India, doing my post-graduate studies in psychology. I was introduced to privately circulated newsletters and magazines that opened a whole new world to me. I loved every bit of the feminist writings by women and the different streams of thoughts. These writings connected me to many women across the country, from Kolkata to Mumbai and from Delhi to Hyderabad to Bangalore. This gave me new strength and vigour to face the challenges of my life with hope and positivity. I began to understand the word 'patriarchy' and how it manifested itself in daily life. It validated my thoughts that I was not alone in finding traditional culture suffocating. I felt empowered by the views of other women who were expressive, daring, and rebellious, struggling for self-respect and dignity for all women in a just society. When I expressed my new found 'knowledge and wisdom' to my parents, they were visibly disapproving and told me that I was in the wrong circle of friends and on the wrong path.

Accidental Marriage and Divorce

During this phase, I met a handsome, intelligent man who believed in the democratic ideals which were beginning to fascinate me – equality, justice, liberty for all. It was an instant appeal, and we became friends. I was in my mid-twenties and he was my first male friend. My parents got wind of it and accepted him because they were surprised that I liked someone. Unfortunately for us, the pressure from parents to tie the knot began. We reluctantly got married. My life changed dramatically after that. My doctoral studies, which I had begun, got neglected in the process. I was introduced to a difficult existence in the rough and rugged terrain of village life with meagre privileges. After the initial romantic idealism, it proved to be a challenge with my persisting fragile health condition. My husband and I had differences over our lifestyles. He wanted to work at the grass-roots level. Although I savoured the rich experiences of rural social work and the great insights it provided, it was short-lived, and so was the marriage. I wanted a reasonably comfortable life. He wanted a child and I was not prepared, for I felt unsettled and uncertain of my future with him. I decided to quit the village and the relationship as well. He wanted me back on his terms. I stuck to my decision.

Picking Up the Lost Threads

I looked forward to getting back to psychology after a gap of almost five years. From the parched rural village, I shifted to Bombay, a vibrant metropolis in West India, where I felt like the proverbial Rip Van Winkle, who slept for many years and then awoke to a new world that was totally unrecognisable to him.

It was a lonely struggle, dealing with my broken marriage and my uncertain future. Being alone in an unknown metro full of ambitious go-getters was scary. The younger generation was practical, professional, and commercial. There was a wide chasm between the two worlds of commerce and social activism, which I had imbibed in the last decade. The groups of women activists in the city helped me adjust and find shared accommodation with two other single women. One was older than me, who had never married, and the other one was younger than me, who had just stepped out of a violent marriage. Being with them was a graceful relief from loneliness. We shared the apartment and our stories, and became good friends. I was beginning to enjoy my life and have fun. I was learning to be independent in thought and attitude. I was learning to negotiate my life out of miserable troubled waters and looking forward to a better and happy future.

It was comforting to be saddled back into psychology at the University of Bombay, pursuing a pre-doctoral degree. I felt refreshed by the pursuit of knowledge that provided the much-needed anchorage to my lost self. This was the turning point in my life as I was hopeful that I could make a decent career in the field. As I was completing my degree, on my parents' suggestion, I decided to shift to Nagpur, a town in Maharashtra, West India, where my parents lived. I made a steady base with my parents and started my professional career as a psychologist. Over the years, after the initial hiccups, I developed a symbiotic relationship of mutual respect and freedom with my parents. It was a safe haven for me, which helped me flourish. My two siblings played a significant role in providing the much-needed anchor of love, compassion, and tolerance. The family stood behind me like a rock, but the community we lived in looked at me curiously. My marriage, divorce, single status, and struggling career provoked them to gossip. In their eyes, I was an object of misery and pity. My parents and me continued to brave the prejudices of the community we lived in.

Life as a Single Woman

One female neighbour was constantly desirous of marrying me off and would advise my parents about this. One married male neighbour made a direct pass at me for a clandestine intimate relationship. I was shocked at the audacity but kept quiet about it. I learnt to maintain a stoic face as I didn't like ugly scenes. Another married doctor visited my clinic and made a similar offer: "I am willing to satisfy your needs in whichever way you want," he said! I didn't know what he was referring to. Another married man invited me for a travel trip, and when I politely declined it, he was surprised. He said that he believed that I would be "footloose and fancy-free" as a single woman. I swallowed such humiliating experiences and did not react to them. It was revealing of their character and not mine, I consoled myself. A single woman does something to the minds of men. I don't know in what way it impacts them. Looking at it from another perspective, I also felt a sense of shame and humiliation. I buried all those unsavoury moments and went about my clinical practice with single-minded devotion. I had to be financially independent first. I wanted to search for meaning and purpose in my life. I needed to evolve into a higher state of being and not just exist at a boring, mundane level.

Singlehood gave me the opportunity to channel my emotions and my loneliness into more work. However, some significant memories stand out. The most painful was the one that happened during a family marriage. I was not allowed to bless the bride at the wedding pavilion because I was single (only married women can bless the bride, I was informed later). That was a shock that sunk deep into my psyche, shattered my confidence and self-esteem, and made me aware of the deep-rooted biases that operate. It was a lesson I never forgot and I tried to keep away from marriage ceremonies thereafter. They reminded me of my pain. I kept away from friendships with married couples, as the female spouse would feel insecure about my presence. I generally searched for friendship with singles.

My shy and submissive temperament was not an asset for the entrepreneurial journey that I had embarked on. Neither was it beneficial for my singlehood. I had to work hard on my personality to improve my skills and attitudes. With time and experience, I became relatively comfortable with social interactions. I tutored myself into getting rid of stage fright and started delivering wonderful speeches! I also trained myself to be assertive and bold. I had to deal with psychological and social threats alone. I faced much harassment and domination by male residents in the new residential society into which we shifted. I was an easy target because I was single and living with aged parents. They wanted to encroach my parking slot, which I did not allow. They scratched filthy abuse onto my car, all over the bonnet and doors, bribed my driver to keep puncturing my car tyres, and sent obnoxious communications on the building group on WhatsApp. I had to resort to local police protection on two occasions and legal help to stop the onslaught. It made me tougher and a fighter of sorts. It also made a bit of a dent on my social image.

After a gap of several years, in my mid-thirties, I entered a serious friendship with a man which seemed comfortable and promising. He was separated from his wife, and the legal process was on. He was helpful, caring, and intelligent company. For a change, it was comforting to have a man by your side to share your experiences. He made several promises but unfortunately never kept them. Life seemed to be hanging loosely on vague assurances. I was politely putting up with the falsehood and losing out on being genuine and true to myself. The dissonance was becoming detrimental to my mental and spiritual well-being. Gradually we drifted apart without making any noise.

As I grew in status in society, a sort of local celebrity, I became more careful of my social persona. I became wary of people and their gossip. I did not want to share my past with anyone. I was reluctant to say that I was divorced. I declared myself to be 'single.' I developed a rather stern aura around myself that put off people and scared them away. I have often heard the comment "she is very strict." I must have developed my hard outer shell as protective self-defence.

Ridicule, Sarcasm, and Hate Mail

Along with my private practice, I started writing a regular designated column on counselling in the local daily newspaper, which continues to this day. I simultaneously penned another column on women's issues for a decade. As I became more vocal through my writings and speeches, I faced mixed reactions from the audience – while some were appreciative, ridicule and hatred from both women and men were also part of the bouquet. Even my parents were not spared as they faced the brunt of my expressions.

I received hate mail from hundreds of men who were part of a national network of men against women. It was a registered organisation supported and funded by men with paid representatives in cities. They would flood my mailbox whenever they disagreed with the views in my column, and the responses would be rabidly prejudiced. The local representative would phone, provoke me into a discussion, and eventually abuse me. It would make my resolve stronger, for I knew I was touching the raw nerves of men who were doing wrong to women. I continued to maintain my stand with conviction even in the face of adversity when men would tease, rag, or make snide comments on me being a 'single' person. Innocuous insinuations such as 'being miserable,' 'frustrated,' and a 'man-hater' were made. Being a psychologist helped me tremendously in handling such demeaning advances with calmness and equanimity without harming myself emotionally.

The Winds of Change

> On the day when it will be possible for woman to love not in her weakness but in her strength, not to escape herself but to find herself, not to abase herself but to assert herself – on that day love will become for her, as for man, a source of life and not of mortal danger.
>
> Simone de Beauvoir[2]

My practice, as well as my presence in the media, became significant over a period of time. I started receiving recognition for being a woman of substance, a role model for many young, aspiring, career-oriented girls. The feelings of my neighbours changed from pity to respect and pride. I noticed with surprise that I was a source of envy for educated married women who felt their lives were wasted being 'just housewives.' This was just like the 'wheel turning full circle.' In our community, a tragedy struck a family that changed

---

2 Simone de Beauvoir, 1949. Retrieved 22 November 2022. Source: https://www.theguardian.com/books/2014/jan/09/simone-de-beauvoir-google-doodle-quotes

the attitudes of many. A newly married young girl became widowed, and her in-laws sent her back permanently to her parents' home. I played a role in planning her future with further education and a job. With changing times, we could see young girls giving priority to full-time careers and postponing marriage. This provoked anxiety in parents who thought otherwise. In my practice, an increasing number of young girls who were facing difficulty finding compatible grooms due to their career pursuits came to me for consultation. I also witnessed the rise in marital conflict and eventual divorce among the young generation. I was being blamed for encouraging divorce among couples. The older generation was perplexed by the prevailing winds and diagnosed it as the fallout of providing higher education to girls. However, parents of girls also realised the value of higher education as a useful fallback resource in bad times, such as a husband's death or divorce. Still, they did not value full-time career making as a priority over marriage. My clinic offered me a good window from which to observe society. We could see a few young career-oriented women opting for singlehood over marriage. Their growing number was a topic for anxious discussions. But I believe that, while women's attitudes had undergone tremendous change, the attitudes of men had not. The stigma of being a single woman continued.

The Last Leg: A Spiritual Journey

> Each soul is potentially divine. The goal is to manifest this perfection and divinity by controlling nature, external and internal. Do this either by work, or worship, or psychic control, or philosophy – by one, or more, or all of these – and be free...
>
> Swami Vivekananda[3]

---

3 Swami Vivekananda. Retrieved 24 November 2022. Source: https://www.goodreads.com/quotes/68229-each-soul-is-potentially-divine-the-goal-is-to-manifest

Spiritual psychology connects to science and spirituality. It believes in the empowerment of the mind for the evolution of the self and transcendence to a spiritual being. While I helped my clients in psychological healing and personal growth, I helped myself too.

I understood in principle that I have to take care of my own problems of loneliness, depression, struggles, and sorrows. My health predicaments empowered me with compassion for self, empathy, kindness, and self-care. Hence, I never allowed myself to fall into the trap of feeling like a 'victim,' for that would have been detrimental to my physical and mental health. I introspected deeply within myself as a habit and became aware of my emotions and my coping styles. Besides my family, the science of psychology and Vedanta have been the strongest inspirations in my journey.

It was nice to know that the Vedanta never believed that a woman is inferior to a man. In fact, it says each one is divine and has the seeds of potential to grow into a beautiful human. Reading Vedanta philosophy brought more clarity that the power is within me and does not depend on others outside us. No one can make me happy as the fountainhead of happiness is within me. It instilled faith in me that, as a single woman, I can lead my own life with a sense of balance and stability. The philosophy of Vedanta was beautiful and elevating and made me feel complete by myself.

Age and menopause brought calmness in me. I feel comfortable and satisfied with myself. I am quite in control of my body, mind, and intellect. I feel content with what I have accomplished professionally, but I want to continue to work and do more. Today, when people ask me the question "Why are you single?" I give a mysterious smile with a twinkle in my eye! I am what I am. I am single, and I am happy.

*****

Destiny Created the Choice

Anjali Khanna, India

This Was Me!

I grew up in a simple middle-class family of government employees. My grandmother loved us a lot but also pitied us because we did not have a brother. I remember an occasion when I cried a lot on the eve of Raksha Bandhan[1] because I did not want to tie Rakhi to my cousin, who took every chance to belittle us sisters and act high and mighty about the fact that he was a boy, and that his parents gave us much smaller gifts than what they gave to their own daughter, for he was her real brother. Like any other typical middle-class Punjabi family, rules were different for us girls compared to boys. They got away with anything and everything – be it entering the kitchen without having a bath, hanging out on the roads with friends, staying away from home beyond six in the evening, and other such restrictions. Many similar instances made us accept that men are stronger and an integral part of our life. Hence, they should always be put on a higher pedestal, and we cannot survive without them.

---

[1] An Indian festival in which sisters tie Rakhis (decorative threads) on their brothers' wrists.

Nevertheless, the rebel in me wanted to prove the opposite. Hence, as I grew up, I was an independent, strong, loud, work-oriented person wanting to break one stereotype after another to the world outside. To the extent that in my friendship circle, I was now known as one strong, blunt, and outspoken person who would speak what came to her mind. However, somewhere within me, I yearned for approval from my father, wanted to be my cousin brothers' favourite, and sought after a comfortable person to be with amongst my male friends. Their approval mattered a lot.

Short Married Life

My life changed completely when I started dating a nice, sweet, and humble musician from a superstitious family. In the midst of some vague opposition, we got married after eight years of acquaintance plus dating and engagement. Once we got married, in my urge to prove to them that their son had chosen the right girl to get married to, though from a different community, I quickly got trapped into their patriarchal system. I believed I should adjust to their way of life and surrender to their beliefs, traditions, and systems. I started giving up my wishes and desires and reacted less to many of their values and systems (though that was also high in their opinion). My appearance, preferences, and prayers, which are very personal, were in tandem with their thoughts. I changed my life schedule completely to suit my husband's lifestyle, even though it harmed my health. My work schedule was 9 am to 5 pm, and he worked from 7 pm in the evening till 2 or 3 am. I started compromising rest and sleep time to ensure he was comfortable, and took complete responsibility for the household jobs (cooking, cleaning, etc.) to ensure everyone else was peaceful. Though I had a hectic work schedule, the good part was that I could reach in time and travel back comfortably by a chartered bus, which helped me partially catch up with sleep. I withdrew from most of my friends and personal acquaintances without any hesitation since this is what my mother and other ladies in my own family did. We were blessed with a daughter. Life was normal, if not great. We were like any other couple managing our family and our life.

The Sudden Shock

One evening in November my husband felt a bit acidic and collapsed. By the time we managed to take him to the hospital, everything was over. He was no more. His death left me in a state of shock, which a part of me has still not overcome. His death continues to haunt me as the biggest mystery of my life, as he was gone within minutes.

I still ask myself, "aakhir usse hua kya tha?" [what happened to him after all?] I became a single woman after eight years of marriage.

Dealing with Singlehood and Social Reactions

I could not figure out how to handle this new state of singlehood. Reading books like the Ramayana to make me feel closer to God as recommended by older ladies of the family made me feel that widowhood is the curse you live for your past sins, which further took me on a guilt trip. I became suddenly very conscious of how I should speak or express myself. If I laughed, people might think I was not sad about my husband's death; if I cried, I might be trying to gain sympathy. I was scared of dressing up well, thinking that people would judge me – my dialogue with myself increased manifold. Sitting alone and wondering about the bad karmas[2] that have landed me here became a regular feature in life. I tried coping with strength – strength in the outer world but dealing with the weak and lonely part within myself. There were times when I just sat idle, doing nothing for hours, and there were days when I worked too hard, hoping to get so tired that I would crash out and sleep. Some days, I could not sleep properly; I felt scared sharing this with others, wondering what they would infer about my loneliness. Moreover, on days when I slept well, I woke up feeling guilty that my mom-in-law would think that I was not grieving my husband's death.

I still remember an evening when I came home from work and, sitting in the washroom, had a very severe panic attack. I screamed

---

2 This is a Hindi word meaning deeds.

so much and cried so loud that my neighbours came running to our house. I packed all my bright clothes, stopped applying eyeliner, and ceased eating mangoes (which continued for almost 17 years) because my husband liked all that. I was crazy about music, which was one reason I was attracted to him, but I stopped listening to it altogether now that he was gone away. I packed all of the music cassettes I had. All his musical instruments were given in donation, and so were many of his clothes. I got into a state of depression and had to start taking tranquilisers. My six-year-old daughter's friends began asking her why her mother looked so old. People in the office told me that I was looking lost and recommended visiting a salon.

My friends also showed concern about my financial status, and suggestions started pouring in from all directions on how I should lead my life. People felt they were encouraging me, but these only added to my anxieties. Some people in the office straight away asked me if they could be of any financial help. One supposedly very close friend offered some clothes that her daughter had just worn a couple of times. This incident worked as a trigger for me. I made two firm decisions – I would earn my living so well and lead so comfortable a life that people would not pity me because my husband died, and my daughter would never feel that she could not get something because her father was not there.

I was a clean-hearted, outspoken person. Being single now had suddenly also created the fear of other women not being comfortable about their husbands talking to me and doubt about men taking advantage of me. I started distancing myself from all male friends and the spouses of female friends. Furthermore, the once highly extraverted and so-called 'cool Anjali' was replaced by a fearful, less confident person who was no longer one of the arguing type. Somewhere that change has found its place so deep in me that I still get apprehensive about openly communicating my thoughts to everyone comfortably.

Another peculiar thing that I feel about single women in my kind of situation is that we become emotionally vulnerable. This vulnerability is mostly because of the patriarchy, in which a belief is inculcated in us that we cannot do without a man in our life. People can easily manipulate and take advantage of us.

The financial insecurity of running my home alone made me also hesitant to take risks. It took seven years to decide to switch jobs. However, the day I did that, my professional associations widened faster, and I grew professionally much faster.

Experience of Trying to Find a Partner

I gradually started collecting myself. After thinking through my emotions, I made a decision, which was majorly governed by my thought that having a man in life is very important to bring up a child. Thus, I began my journey to find a new husband. One fine afternoon, I threw away all the anti-anxiety pills that I was taking with a determination not to touch them ever again. I restarted going for walks to become physically better. I visited the salon and gradually started taking out my packed-away clothes.

Some people approached my mother with the proposition of an alliance but on the condition that I would have to send my daughter to a residential school. I told them to get lost. I registered myself on a matrimonial site with the help of a friend and his wife. This was yet another experience of dealing with men. I saw men of my age group with diabolic personalities. They wanted the lady to either look after their child or be willing to produce a child for them, but no discussion ever happened around my child. However, I was here to find a father for my daughter. Finally, I came across a man who said, "you deserve to be loved and looked after," "it will be tough to bring up your daughter alone," "you need to have a man in your life," "people are selfish," and "you are young and need a companion." I started falling for him from day one. In our first meeting, he spoke about my daughter and my family, about my career and how I should develop further, and what not. I started feeling he was the right man for me. But he was a flirt and connected with multiple women through matrimony, friendship, or other professional network sites. Most of them were given some hope, professional or personal, because of which they kept connected to him. He did not hesitate to flirt with other women in my presence, which I took lightly, thinking that he meant no harm. I saw some messages which were directly sexual in nature that he had sent to some women. When I objected to them, he would give me some explanation, which I accepted. I was shocked when I saw an exchange of messages between him and his wife's niece, which did not look like messages from an uncle to his niece. After a few years of being with him, I became aware that the man was already married and lived in the same house with his wife (happy or not). I got alarmed when my daughter alerted me one day of his advances towards her. I also found out that he was going through financial problems – and having taking advantage of my emotional state, he had managed to fool me out of a few lakhs. This episode made me realise that I was not as strong emotionally as I had always thought I was. I went through days of uncertainty, nervousness, and feeling cheated before I finally decided to put an end to this relationship firmly. All his messages, calls, and apologies, direct or indirect, were ignored.

An Emerging New Person

With more than 18 years of singlehood, I have changed drastically with time. I have matured with age, become open about many things. I do not judge people for certain things that are outside the stereotypes of society. In the last ten years or so, I read a lot, joined many professional forums, made many friends, and concluded that I do not need a man to lead my life. I am a self-reliant and independent woman who likes to be happy. I have shed many apprehensions in life, thanks to some of the excellent gurus (teachers) I have had, including my daughter. I am professionally well-placed, emotionally more in charge of myself, and not looking for a man to lead a peaceful and happy life anymore – though nor have I closed the doors on that possibility. I have made lots of friends professionally and personally (and have also lost a few). I do not feel any apprehension when I am talking to any men in the office, or among family and friends. I do all I want to do, have studied and completed my MBA and certifications in management, and have established a strong network which helps me boost myself whenever I am low. I cannot say things are perfect, but nor were they even when my husband was around.

Where Am I Today?

Everything in life happens with a purpose. I believe that all I have gone through in the last 18 years was also to help me grow into a much stronger individual. My life today has changed for the better. I have become a much more successful, joyful, and enjoyable person. Today I am looking after myself well and have succeeded in raising my daughter as a highly independent person. I look after my parents well and support my siblings in the best possible manner. I have reconnected myself to everything I left after my husband's death, most significantly to music and this time with greater intensity and passion. I have no regrets in life, though the question still lingers on about how everything can change in the spur of a second.

Some feeling of insecurity still lingers on. I am still scared of taking too much professional risk, not very confident, and hesitate to speak or challenge my employers in the fear of losing my job. The fear of not being able to manage if I do not have a source of earning has been and remains my biggest fear. I have been living with my parents and daughter till now. At 52, the fear of living alone is also cropping up as my parents are old, and my daughter's future might take her to some other place. I make efforts to be overly independent and do not want to come between my daughter and her dreams.

Despite all this, I have immense gratitude for life. I am bringing out my highest potential – and *I am happy*.

*****

Reclaiming Myself – Realising My Dreams

Tangil Smith, USA

Overview

I am an African American single woman in the United States, determined to follow my dreams and aspirations after breaking free from an oppressive marriage.

My preference for only dating African American men did not always yield the desired results. African American men satisfied my primal senses (sight, touch, smell, taste, and sound); however, my personality type, core values, or love languages were unsatisfied. I have had numerous conversations with African American women, both married and single, who share the same sentiment and recognise the shortage of good men within this category. Research has shown, and most African American women believe, that dating an African American male is nearly impossible due to imprisonment, unemployment, criminal activity, sexual orientation, or racial preference. Imagine the limitations, challenges, and damage if my preference was dating African American men.

Also, working in corporate America, I found myself overworked, overcommitted, and unsatisfied. My attempts to find my dating preference amongst those with my level of work experience, intellect, and passions left me with insufficient options. Ultimately, I decided to build a relationship with myself while waiting on 'The One.'

After the past five years of being divorced, with each stride, I find more satisfaction in focusing on my self-awareness, self-development, and self-care, which fills the void I'd been searching to fill with a romantic relationship.

I have slowly transitioned from pointless dating to seriously investing more time in developing myself. The reality is, becoming more self-aware helped me remove the veil from what I had buried, ignored, and was oblivious to. The epiphany here is that my self-development is changing the trajectory of my learnt life template, as set by my parents. I find myself growing out of the box and boundaries of that social environment. The action of performing self-care is drawing me to a deeper meaning of life and making my relationship with myself a love affair like I've never known before. It may sound like bliss, and it can be; however, it did not begin this way for me. I have found that focusing on my overall well-being is a process, and with every victory also came a multitude of failures; but in the end, it has been entirely worth it.

The Template

My parents' template had a significant influence on my relationship outlook. In 1968, my parents, barely 21 and 22 years old, were boundless and courageous enough to leave their home and family in Mississippi, and move to Northern California. Their focus was on creating a better life for themselves and their children. When I reflect on my relationship outlook, I have understood my parents' template as: put God first, make an inviting and loving home for your family, support and encourage your spouse, teach your children to respect themselves and others, serve your community (work and church) through servant leadership, and with whatever is left, you can spend time on yourself. These mantras were shown and taught to my siblings and me directly by my parents in my adolescent years.

I get my tenacity and confidence from my dad and my strength and positivity from my mom. Dad focused on work and more work, and when he was not working, he was hanging out playing basketball, ping-pong, dominoes, and cards with his best friend, my uncle. His philosophy was, 'work hard, play hard.' When he spent time with us, it usually involved us going with him to hang out with his friends. My brothers and I participated in many activities and quickly learned how to be competitive and strategic while playing games. Dad brought an energising presence that often overshadowed Mom's dedicated daily efforts of supporting the family in the home. When I got the chance for alone time with Dad, it would include eagerly listening to life lessons and his infamous quotes, such as "strive to be number one," "you can be anything you want to be," and "there's nothing to it but to do it." Spending time with Dad always left you feeling like you could accomplish anything.

Furthermore, my mother also worked, but she loved preparing a beautiful home filled with an abundance of love and support. Mom showed us that helping others, even before yourself, was the way of life. Though her heart and intent were noble, I saw a pattern of constant complaining regarding Dad being absent as her partner in the marriage. Dad worked at night and wasn't often physically present, but he prided himself on paying the bills. There were many nights I saw Mom cry while we watched our favourite TV shows together. I never imagined that while she was serving others, she was in desperate need of love, care, and support.

By the time I was 15 years old, I had realised the lack of love, respect, and even romance in my parents' marriage, and I vowed not to have the same fate. It motivated me to set goals for college; I wanted to become a dancer and travel the world. My parents never went to college, so they did not understand or support my wish to go away to the Julliard School in New York City. Instead, they paid for me to go to the local community college down the street. After my dreams of going away to college were unfulfilled, becoming a dancer at the local community college did not give me the same sense of purpose, and going to school seemed pointless. I needed an escape while living at home and found refuge either at work or the local dance clubs. The reality of not leaving home was discouraging and eventually changed the course of my life.

As a young adult at home, I paid more attention to my parents' relationship. I knew I wanted the opposite of what I saw in their marriage: Mom constantly cooking and cleaning, Dad always gone, and plenty of arguments in between. I associated Mom's unhappiness with being a housewife. All she did was take care of everyone else's needs before her own; she was self-less. I resented her for not commanding what she wanted and deserved; therefore, I was determined not to be like her. I focused on being a corporate professional instead of a housewife like my mother. I believed that by working, I could be less dependent on a man, and more of a corporate businesswoman, commanding respect, love, and support. Over time, I unconsciously adopted my father's work habits, always working and never home.

When it was time for marriage, I decided to choose someone the opposite of my dad. I thought, "My man will support me emotionally; he will be romantic, more of a partner who helps cook, clean, and is actively visible in raising his family."

Blue Moon

As I joined the workforce at the age of 19, I worked for an airline carrier that flew from San Francisco to Honolulu, Hawaii weekly, and I had a fantastic employee discount. I was doing well, saved my money, and set off for a vacation with a girlfriend to Hawaii. We were amazed at the nice weather, everyone seemed happy, there were night clubs open until 6 a.m., and gorgeous guys everywhere. On our third night, at two o'clock in the morning, while we were walking the streets of Waikiki taking pictures of people we met along the way, we encountered an attractive guy on Kalakaua Blvd. He was six-foot-three, handsome, and well dressed, and we learned he was a ranking petty officer in the US Army. After some conversation, he walked us back to our hotel at the Maile Sky Court, took my number, and said, "Have you ever seen a blue moon?" I said "no," and his response was, "I will have plans for us tomorrow."

During that week, he was determined to show me a blue moon, white sands, and one of the most romantic evenings I could imagine. The next night, he picked me up for dinner, brought me flowers, opened my door, and had awesome jazz music blaring from his car. It was very grownup stuff for a 19-year-old. At dinner, he ordered our drinks, had us sit in an open space where we could gaze upon the sunset as we listened to the roaring waves of the ocean. We had lots of laughs, engaging conversation, and he asked a ton of questions regarding what I wanted to do with my future.

Afterward, he grabbed my hand and said, "I want to show you something." He led me right onto the beautiful sandy beach, and as the fall breeze blew across my face, he told me how beautiful and captivating I was as the blue moon reflected in his eyes. This experience felt like a movie, my heart was full of passion and love, or so I thought. He came down from the Schofield barracks every day to see me until I went back to California. Shortly after that, I went back for a weekend to see him again, followed by him visiting me in California for two weeks. Never did I imagine that on my trip, I would bring back the man I would marry.

Marriage

Yes, this man I married was handsome, suave, and a smooth talker. He swept my young starry-eyed self to the marriage altar before I processed all the red flags in between. It wasn't immediate, however. After two years of dating, we were married on 24 April 1988. At this point, passion overshadowed my desire to go away to college, so I dropped out.

After getting married, I learned that the fairy tales of marriage filled with heart-warming hugs and kisses like in the Doris Day movies were not a reality. Nor were there passionate dances between lovers like Fred Astaire and Ginger Rogers. We had constant conflict, frustration, and hurtful and painful words that almost broke my spirit. Occasionally there was a flicker of happiness for a couple of months, then the flame would die, and we'd go back to agony; the results of this marriage template began to seem familiar.

Over seven years of marriage we experienced many ups and downs, from dealing with the highs and lows of his gambling addiction, to his jealousy at my business success. We argued and fought all the time, even over household chores (such as cooking, cleaning, and washing). Never had I experienced such frustration. Only two months after our wedding day, I got pregnant and I was devastated. I did not want to have a child with him because our lives were so full of drama and discord. At that time, I believed I hated him. I contemplated abortion and even made an appointment twice, but because of my religious beliefs, I held myself back from doing so.

Approximately five-and-a-half months into the pregnancy, I finally began to accept that I would be a mom in four months or less. It did not negate the fact that I was extremely unhappy and strongly felt we should divorce, even if it meant raising the child alone. His regular pattern was to take the car on Friday and come home Sunday, but this time, I had had enough. There I sat, pregnant, in my childhood bed at my parents' house, feeling like a complete idiot. When he finally came home Sunday after midnight, we had a horrible argument; eventually, he calmed me down, and I went to sleep. Less than two hours later, I was having contractions and unbearable pain; it was alarming, so my husband and parents rushed me to the hospital. Yes, it was happening; in just a few hours, I was going to birth a premature baby weighing one pound and nine ounces. On the way to the hospital, I prayed that God would be with me during this time, and my spirit was calm. The comforting presence I felt from the Holy Spirit assured me I would be alright but warned me that the baby would not be. I was prepared for the worst. After four hours of pushing and screaming, baby Mack was born. He looked just like my husband, and he was long, but I noticed that his eyes were not open and he was gasping for air. He lived only five minutes and six seconds; his lungs were not fully developed, and there was no advanced technology back then that could save him. The nurses took pictures, wrapped him up, and took him to the morgue. The next day I requested that he be wrapped up as if he were sleeping and brought to my bedside, as I suspected that I wouldn't be having another child with this man. He looked as if he was in peaceful sleep; I had visitors and they began to whisper, wondering if I understood that the baby was not alive. I fully knew he wasn't. I kept him with me until he began to thaw and turn a little blue. My heart was satisfied that I got a chance to spend time with this being that I had carried for five-and-a-half months. Two days after, we buried baby Mack in what looked like a shoebox, and I was back to work the following Monday. It was the most traumatic thing I had ever experienced. At the age of 23, this was unbearable; I wanted a divorce, but, at this point, the need to console one another was greater than the desire to leave the marriage.

My husband blamed himself for baby Mack's passing, saying "If I had not stressed you out…," and I spent the bulk of that time helping him to heal. The battle that caused most of our stress was his gambling addiction, which affected everyone. Eventually, I talked him into going to Gamblers Anonymous while I went to Gam-Anon.[1] I was furious that I had to be there; it felt as if I were being punished for his problem.

He stopped going after two sessions. With a life-altering traumatic experience and an identified addict as a husband, I began to turn to alcohol and cigarettes. I was not a fan of either and eventually found solace in food, gaining more weight than when we first met. I felt stuck, which turned to hopelessness, and I stopped taking care of myself, spiralling into the lowest level of depression I had ever known. I went through a series of emotional struggles and didn't know how to change my situation.

---

1 Gamblers Anonymous is a support group of men and women who have a desire to stop gambling; Gam-Anon is a support group of men and women affected by a friend or loved one who is addicted to gambling.

Seven years later, I filed for divorce, which was extraordinarily freeing. At 29, I set out on a path of catching up on the dreams that I hadn't had the mental capacity to begin. That included finishing college, making my own financial decisions, and losing all the weight I had gained. It felt great to be free of all marriage trauma and drama for that year and a half; however, I missed being with him sexually, as he was the only man I'd known for seven years. Therefore, in the spirit of 'one last time,' one week before the divorce was final, we set a date to meet in Capitola.

We had such a great day. We had dinner, walked along Capitola Beach, laughed, talked, and reminisced about how we first met. Little did I know he had plans for me: he was intending to get me pregnant. True to his plan, this innocent church girl found herself pregnant by her ex-husband. It felt like a Jerry Springer moment. Our second child came nine months later.

A year later, we remarried, raising our second son in our second marriage. It was natural to believe that this was a second chance for us, and we declared that we would be a better couple for our son. Over the next seven years, life was initially better, and raising our son was our primary objective. I did not anticipate, given all we had overcome, that the new thing we would argue over would be how to raise a male child. At this point, the goal I had made for myself had become buried and eventually cast into the abyss of my memory. My focus was solely on working in a corporate environment that paid top dollar, managing the family household, performing servant leadership at church, and being a good mother. Eventually, I gained 125 pounds, which resulted in low self-esteem, and was on a fast track to being a workaholic.

I had no work–life balance, but it became an acceptable way of life. I gained fulfilment working and told myself that maybe that is why I am here, not for myself but to support my husband and son. As I reflect, I think, "what a load of cow manure, this is how my mother used to be." I was beginning to accept that my feelings and existence were unimportant. I didn't realise that I was living on autopilot during these challenging times, and the light within had gone from dim to dark.

According to Linda Berens, "an inaccurate type of pattern often becomes the story the people tell themselves about who they are." I told the story and whole-heartedly believed it.[2]

In 2008, we were affected by a reduction in the workforce. My husband was more challenged coping than I. He returned to his old habits and ways of being, chauvinistic beliefs, new gambling debts, and newly surfaced personality disorders. Eventually, this behaviour led to the end of our marriage, and my 17-year-old son and I moved out. A year later, my son went away to college, and I spent the next three years living like a hermit until I eventually filed for a divorce.

I had neglected myself for so long, I didn't know what I was passionate about anymore, nor did I know what I wanted out of life. As I embrace my journey today, the reality is that a true love story of the most significant magnitude is revealed the more self-aware I become.

Since the divorce, I have realised I keep creating ways to progress, either within my corporate life or my side businesses. In times of reflection, I have concluded that this drive to make a better life for myself and my son also comes from my parents' template. Furthermore, it gives me a sense of purpose, instant gratification, and a feeling of self-satisfaction. Although rewarding, I have also discovered that chasing these ambitions leaves me mentally exhausted and often lonely.

My Epiphany

For the first three years, being alone after the divorce, I vowed that my focus would be on me and what I wanted. I told myself there

---

2 Linda Berens, *The Self-discovery Process* (2013). Retrieved 10 September 2021. Source: https://lindaberens.com/resources/methodology-articles/the-self-discovery-process

would be no dates, no conversations, simply me hiding under the cloak of Jesus. After spending ridiculous amounts of money on expensive furniture, fine dining, clothes, unused gym memberships, and international travel trips, I still was not satisfied. I did not know what the hell I wanted or where to start. Surprisingly, the actual quest for self-development was beginning.

I came to accept that my original dream of dancing as a profession was over; my knees and feet riddled by arthritis and body plagued with diabetes limited my range of motion. The good news was I could still travel, go back to college, and finish what I started. These were some of my original goals, and it felt great that I had the mental capacity to focus on getting it done. Though I had this goal to go back to school, the idea of dating was slowly creeping into my thoughts. As I opened my eyes to the things around me, I became energised, and I wanted to date, to explore being courted and romanced. I started with swiping right on every dating site. The process involved looking at tons of digital profiles of African American men that described their interests, hobbies, and backgrounds, resulting in approximately 25 responses, ten conversations, and half a dozen in-person dating moments.

Laughing out loud at myself, I realise I had made this an experiment, looking for patterns in each man I talked to. I developed a process that involved three text messages, phone screenings, and eventually a face-to-face date. It was very much like recruiting, looking for the right candidate. I chose to meet these dates at a restaurant I often frequented – the manager knew me by first name and it felt safe. This was becoming commonplace: blind dates, friends setting me up with friends of friends, and of course, online dating apps. I was so excited to date, especially since I had missed the whole dating experience as an adult.

A girlfriend of mine, single for more than 40 years, told me, "know what you want, and be clear in communicating what you need, and if you can't do that, don't play with the big dogs, stay your ass on the porch." Later I learned she was right. The year of my divorce, I started dating before I knew what I needed, and I thought I was in love. It was far from that, and I still hadn't spent any time developing who I wanted to be. A male friend once said, "it's like you've been in a petrified forest for years, and now everything is luscious and green." As funny as that sounded, it was sad but true.

As a result, I engaged a life coach who introduced me to new ways of thinking, and he held me accountable for considering my needs before others. My coach drilled me weekly on things below the surface. This line of questioning was so foreign that I often tried to deflect and, in some cases, didn't know how to answer. My self-burial blinded me; at times, I couldn't think of a response. Part of this development process was to work on the things below the surface, such as why I neglected myself, why I stress ate, why I worked so much, and why I often spoke negative messages to myself.

At this point, I was nearly 50, and I had never said out loud or believed that I was beautiful. I didn't realise what a poor self-image I had carried for so many years. When my coach would call, he'd ask, "how are you?" Naturally, I'd smile and say, "I'm fine," and then he'd reply, "when will you stop lying to yourself?" I found this offensive, considering that I saw myself as a woman of integrity and honour. What did he mean by lying to myself? Taking this time to self-develop and uncover my truth was challenging and eye-opening. I could no longer bury my feelings working with this coach, nor could I focus on pleasing others knowingly. He unlocked positive energy I had not experienced since I was in my late teens. The clear message here was to focus on self-development. The only relationship that was paramount was the one I was forming from within.

Self-care

According to Ashley Mateo, "When you're not legally bound to another person, you have the freedom to learn, grow, and explore, without any of the guilt associated with taking time for self-care."[3]

Now a middle-aged African American single woman, I find myself in relationship discussions, which are often based around both genders being frustrated with the entire dating scene. Usually, the conversation is about dating amidst Covid-19, how no one really wants to meet in person, how educated women cannot find men financially suitable as mates, or how good men cannot find committed women who will settle for a man with an average income because of her level of success. A thought to ponder: "where does that leave me?" Though I am wishful to date my preference, how many will I find in my social circle? My age group competes with women that are younger, more athletic, and overall willing to sell themselves for money. I ask myself, if I don't have the brickhouse body I once had, I'm not as fast-moving because of my ailments, and I don't need a man's money, what type of mate is there for me? Should I consider other ethnicities and cultures, or less-educated men, or those with less money? These internal conversations resulted in a loud and clear voice saying, "Girl, you better focus on yourself." These messages are referring to self-care.

Furthermore, over the last five years, I have fought to think of my needs and wants first, pursuing my goals and dreams while not losing focus on finishing what I started; hence, I went back to school. I was tired of being told in a condescending voice, "you've done well for yourself without a degree." I used this type of statement as fuel to show others that I didn't need a degree to be accepted. I defied being put into a box or labelled as someone who can't achieve. The

---

3 Ashley Mateo, 'The surprising benefits of being single,' Oprah Daily (26 March 2021). Retrieved 9 September 2021. Source: https://www.oprahdaily.com/life/relationships-love/a27790346/benefits-of-being-single/#:~:text=When%20you're%20not%20legally,are%20and%20what%20you%20owant

truth is, I sacrificed my goals for my husband and son and wasn't sure what degree to pursue.

With my new awareness, I took time to build on what was important to me. I realised that for me to feel confident and accomplished, I needed to finish what I had begun. I graduated in May of 2020 with a bachelor of science degree in industrial/organisational psychology. After 36 years of helping everyone else, I finally achieved another one of my original goals, an unbelievable achievement during Covid-19. The driving force that kept me determined was that I wanted to show my son that it is never too late to achieve your goals.

Not only this, but I am also still hoping to dance again; however, my weight has impacted my self-image and physical well-being. Currently, I am saddled with Type 2 diabetes and arthritis in my knees and feet, which limit my ability to have a full range of motion. My focus now is to lose 100 of the pounds I gained during my marriage. I worked on getting to the root cause of why I ended up here in the first place, and I am still soul searching. Taking an introspective look at my choices, I realise that I changed after I got married. I changed from being active outdoors to sedentary and indoors. Doing self-development and self-discovery has led me to designing a roadmap that will guide me from self-loathing to a place of joy, peace, and self-satisfaction. To date, I have lost 40 pounds with a goal of 85 pounds to go. I believe this is the key to catapulting me into inner peace.

Reflection

Again, for the first time, I feel like my life's journey is my own to create. I wanted to increase my chances of growing and not becoming old and complacent, and I recently moved to the big city of Atlanta, Georgia. Within my social circles, Atlanta has the reputation of being filled with African Americans thriving as entrepreneurs and business professionals. This environment supports my race, culture, and growth mindset. I look forward to seeing what new things I discover about myself while here.

In conclusion, my journey now is not about finding someone to complete me or even reaching the destination of marriage. It's about discovering my God-given talents and using them in the Universe. Planning how I will learn, achieve, and nurture what lies beneath the surface of what I show the world. As I walk this life and challenges arise, the list of questions to answer includes: is this a new awareness of self – what template am I following? Is self-development needed? What is the root cause of what I see? Do I need self-care? Am I growing and being productive in the goals I have created? Continually asking these questions of myself allows for a quick self-check. I am holding myself accountable while embracing the journey. Every day I learn something new about what gives me peace, love, and security. I'm creating the life I've always wanted and deserved.

*****

Becoming Whole… Singly

Priya Vasudevan, India

Mixed Messages and Polarity

Growing up, I was a fan of romantic movies, especially Hollywood ones. If you are also a fan of this genre, you will recall Tom Cruise in *Jerry McGuire* saying to Renée Zellweger, "You complete me!" Either through such iconic movies or Indian mythological stories, the concept of male and female together forming a 'whole' was part of my social conditioning while growing up. My parents, however, gave me mixed messages: "Stand on your own feet!" and "Earn your own living. Don't be dependent," but also, "Marry as per family choice. Young girls always choose wrong," and "You can behave this way here, but they [the in-laws] won't tolerate all this." As Malayali migrants to the then Maharashtrian-dominated Mumbai, they held on to South Indian tradition: temple visits, Bharatnatyam classes, and all vacations in Kerala only. But the big city fostered modern life: an independent thought process and a resilient spirit.

Growing up as Independent, Achieving, and Responsible

As the oldest child of my parents, my childhood was about academic excellence while sustaining our South Indian roots. Father put my siblings and me in an English-medium school where the sharpest focus was on 'marks,' 'percentage,' and 'rank.' The assumption was that a good education is the key to a prosperous future. While my mother chose to be a homemaker, my early memories are of elders asking me, "What would you like to become when you grow up?" I felt rather important, and a dream took root unconsciously to become somebody of repute and importance. Ambition and middle-class values were blending to become a potent mix. Mother rather naïvely thought that a "good education and a good job result in attracting a well-settled husband," which was the equivalent of a comfortable life. As I saw my mother effortlessly playing the conventional daughter, wife, and mother roles, this became the minimum and almost a given in my mind. However, my efforts were to be more than that. I wanted to be admired as a successful career person who is professional. Steps to achieve that dream took up much of my time in my youth. I qualified to be a pharmacist and later did my MBA in human resource management. Foremost on my mind was, "How do I rise above the ordinary at work and thus in life?"

During a time when being a working woman meant being a secretary or a clerk, I was the youngest female manager at Duphar Interfran Ltd. By that time, my father had retired and I took on the role of family provider. This role involved more than just financial support. My opinion was sought in everything from what my mother will make for dinner to which engineering college my brother should choose. This was confusing for a 23-year-old who was moving too quickly into the role of Karta [head-of-household] from that of being an obedient daughter. As a result, those years also developed a capacity for decision-making, clarity in thinking, and being a nurturer, which would stand me in good stead during future years.

Family Hunt for Grooms

Twenty-three was also the age when Indian parents start searching for suitable grooms for their daughters. As I had, by design, dutifully resisted potential suitors during my college and early career days, my parents decided on the best approach for getting me married. By then, I had developed a more defined sense of self. I was self-assured, economically independent, well-travelled, articulate, and ambitious. The whole idea of the 'boy' and his family coming home to see the 'girl' felt old fashioned to me. The boy's family would evaluate skin tone, physical build, and behavioural leanings (read obedience) of the girl, and I was not a killer in any of these categories. I was seen as wheatish, thin, and outspoken rather than fair, slim, and articulate. These judgements might have been true for others, but for me, they triggered a rebellious streak. I was outraged at being judged by people who were clearly less modern than me.

Every time a suitable 'boy' came into my life and it didn't work out for some reason (whether his or mine), it resulted in either disappointment or relief, as the case might be. My way of coping with such pressures was to excel in work and be recognised for my performance. Work took me to other countries, and my college friends would enviously hear my stories of foreign lands, while global colleagues would admire my capabilities, clothes, and culture. At a time when global folks were revered, or even feared, in multinational corporations, the young me got mentored. This laid the foundation for continuous learning and trusting relationships with senior colleagues.

Another phenomenon that was happening was that available bachelors were fast becoming ineligible. Most of them were starting their careers, while I was already in middle management with a widening salary gap between us. Many of them were not as educated or ambitious as I was. What stood out for me was that I couldn't meet my match. For me, marriage meant a life-long commitment, and I chose to remain single for however long it takes rather than settling for social, physical, or future needs. I knew there would be trade-offs to this choice and I was prepared. Yet deep down, I thought I would get married someday when I met a man I could love and respect at the same time.

As I moved from my early 20s to my late 20s, and then from my early 30s to my late 30s, the responses to my single status in social settings changed from, "So, who will be the lucky guy? Do you have somebody?" to "You will need to scale down your expectations. Marriage is all about compromise" and "You will need somebody in your old age," and then to awkward silences, pitiful glances, and quick changes of topic. I learnt to deal with these responses through humour, self-depreciation, smart comebacks, and often quiet acceptance. Social gatherings were not fun anymore, and I started withdrawing from social circles, becoming reclusive, and avoiding spaces where couples hang out.

Stepping Out and Living Alone

In my mid-30s, I bought my own house and, finally cutting the cord, moved into it. It was emotionally wrenching to step out of a cocoon and expose my vulnerability and singlehood to society. But I needed my own space, and perhaps members of my family needed it too. My parents supported this decision to pre-empt acrimonious scenes in the future, though it broke their hearts. Father felt he had failed in his duty to get me married. Mother assuaged him by saying that at least I was independent and doing well.

In my new home, my neighbours were an old couple, which felt comforting. Slowly, I started forging bonds with people in my housing society. As this was a new building, members of the society were new to each other. There was no previous baggage. They accepted my singlehood as a matter of fact without delving into my past. There were no hints or pieces of advice on marriage. My parents would often visit, and they helped me socialise. However, I was still feeling vulnerable – the neighbourhood shopkeepers asked if I was renting and working in a call centre. The lecherous gaze that accompanied their questions conveyed the stereotype in their mind of single women. I strived hard to be differentiated. Walking with my head and shoulders up and always making eye contact were some of the strategies that kept strangers at bay. I often wondered what would make me feel safe, and my instinctive response was: more power. I volunteered for and was quickly accepted as a committee member in my housing society. The most powerful group in the society became my peers, which left me feeling secure and strong. My opinions made a difference, and I voiced them despite my lack of experience in such matters. People who lived there – from neighbours to security staff, the *paperwallah* [newspaper man] and *milkwallah* [milkman] – saw me as powerful. I was used to this in my office, but experiencing it in social settings felt new and comforting.

Corporate life was a different world altogether. Everything came naturally to me there: attention, acknowledgement, progress, adulation, and even power. Colleagues came to me often as a go-to person for advice, bringing to the surface my potential to nurture. I got several awards in the organisations that I worked for as well as from the human resources industry. My most cherished was the National Award for Innovative Human Resources & Training Practices conferred by the Indian Society of Training & Development (ISTD).

The blend of nurturing and excellence qualities in me often led to curious questions from well-meaning colleagues. They would ask me questions like, "How is a nice girl like you still single?" That made me wonder, what is society's image of a single woman? Perhaps independent, competitive, aggressive, and manipulative or sad, lonely, and deprived. At times, I started to experience a lack of companionship and security. I yearned for somebody who would always be there for me as an equal partner. Most of my friends got married, and then they vanished from my social radar for at least the first couple of years of their married life. I remember killing many holidays simply because I didn't have anybody to go with. I would volunteer to take up any work during festivals as I was the only one on the team who didn't have 'household' responsibilities.

One incident during this period that stands out was a conversation with a complete stranger. I was attending a training programme at the Club Andheri and the facilitator had invited a speaker. This speaker, a senior gentleman, interacted with the participants for a couple of hours and joined us for lunch. At lunch, I chose a seat next to him, and an interesting conversation ensued. Mid-conversation, he politely inquired about what my husband does, to which I replied, "I am single." That led to an awkward pause and then some inconsequential conversation. Towards the end, he looked into my eyes with paternalistic sympathy and said, "I see so much sadness in you!" The authenticity and care with which he said it blocked any retorts that I would have made to such a statement. A stranger who did not know anything of my life felt empowered to say this, due to years of conditioning to believe that being single is not out of choice, and hence worthy of sympathy and judgement.

The more I searched for an equal partner, the more such a person became elusive. But then another array of friends started filling in the gaps in my life through their presence in times I needed them the most – whether it was while moving into a new home, seeing a good movie, going shopping, or when my younger sister got married before me (something that was unheard of at that time).

Thrills and Risks as a Single Woman Traveller

It was at this time that I decided to see the world, irrespective of my lack of companion. Work took me to many states of India as well as to other countries. Wherever I travelled, I made a point of spending some time to see the place as a tourist. A particularly enjoyable detour was the one to Egypt after a meeting in Dubai. A week's trip to see the pyramids, mummies, and the land of ancient pharaohs was scintillating, and I planned it on my own. Landing in Cairo and getting into a cab, then travelling with a guide for the rest of the stay, it all seemed quite bold for that day and age. Curio shopping in street markets was interesting too. In one, the female shopkeeper asked about my marital status and, on hearing that I was single, sold me a papyrus painting, saying that if I kept this at home, "love will find you."

However, it was not all fun – there were some anxious times too. I lost my wallet, which contained my business card – in itself, hardly a loss. However, within a few days, I started getting calls every 15 minutes from unknown numbers. All of them asked for me by name and wanted to know when I would be free to meet. The calls were incessant at night. I started not taking the calls from unknown numbers. As this was my official number, on which I was used to receiving calls from colleagues who were not on my contact list, I was in a pickle. Sometimes, after the calls had seemed to abate, I would think the danger had passed and pick up an unknown call only to be confronted with a lecherous caller. My male colleagues started noticing and took up cudgels on my behalf – till one of the callers told them that my number was listed on a 'call girl' website! In spite of their well-meaning advice to change my number, I refused to part with my first mobile number and kept on ignoring or giving 'wrong number' responses. Steadily, that phase passed too.

Pursuing Life beyond Work

During my mid-30s, a few of my close friends got divorced – some having been cheated on by their husbands while others had become disillusioned with the institution of marriage. Marital responsibilities and then post-marriage discord had paused some of my friendships. However, all of them reconnected – perhaps I was the only friend available who had time (with no family to take care of) to listen to their stories. These stories demystified the social construct of marrying for perpetuity, security, and love. I learnt that people fall out of love. I became more appreciative of my strengths and uniqueness. I felt less lonely and more complete in myself – albeit, this is a life-long journey. I also found myself having a lot of time on my hands – and didn't feel excited about devoting all of it into work or mindless television and movie watching. Being an avid reader, by then, I had accumulated a commendable collection of books across genres, which I treasure to this day. However, simply reading books didn't seem enough. The art of movement, culturally moored, re-awakened during this time. Trained in Bharatnatyam in childhood, I signed up for a course in Mohiniattam – the graceful dance form from Kerala. My guru agreed to teach me the art in one-to-one lessons on Sunday mornings. The gentle, graceful, and artful form consumed me. I would replay the dance moves in my mind, which gave me respite during boring and long-drawn-out meetings, and the lessons were a nice way to spend my Sunday mornings, lasting for several years. Over seven years, I performed Mohiniattam at several social settings in India and abroad.

Being raised in a devout South Indian family, religion was close to my heart. With Hinduism as an anchor, I started moving into the spiritual realm and, after exploration, found that spirituality is the underlying base of any religion. My curiosity to know more about the meaning of life and what awaits in the after-life led me to past-life regression (PLR) work. This became another area where I was fast accumulating knowledge through devouring books on the subject. After around ten books on past lives, PLR became an abiding passion.

My singlehood had been a good space and I was comfortable with it, but I did want to experience life fully, and being a wife and a mother is an important part of that for me. Learning about my past life gave a new meaning to the words 'soulmate' and 'soul families.' I decided that I wanted to find my soulmate. My parents were getting old and their constant refrain – "how do we move on from this world peacefully, knowing that you are alone?" – became a source of worry too. A possibility came up to my liking, and I decided to get married. In my short span of marriage so far, I have discovered that my strong sense of self, developed during singlehood, has enabled me to create a partnership of interdependence – financial and emotional.

Gift of Singlehood

Getting married and having kids seems so preordained in society, almost like an extension of growing up – and for most people it is. But having lived a predominantly single life, I often reflect on what this phase of my life has gifted me. A more secure sense of self, for one thing – I am self-assured, decisive, responsible, and resilient. What has been the trade-off? Having biological children.

As I navigate through life ahead, I look back at my singlehood with gratitude for shaping me into the person I am, for the successes and prosperity that came with it, and for the multitude of friends who became as close as family – encouraging and enabling me to be 'whole.'

*****

Of Freedom and Fairy Tales

Mukta Kamplikar, India

When I came to Pune I recall, that one of my friends was helping me to socialise. A family invited us for breakfast. When I was being introduced to a Maharashtrian Family, I put out my hand and introduced myself, saying, "Hi, I am Mukta," and almost instantly, one of the older gentlemen in the family asked me in Marathi – "Mukta kon / *konachi kon ahes tu*"? [who do you belong to?]. It suddenly struck me that the noun 'Mukta' meant nothing without being attached to a surname or, more specifically, a man. It was an instant reminder that to be attached or belong to someone is 'identity' in many people's minds. Or maybe it is the first thing that people look for. I was reminded that a father's or husband's name is not just a passport requirement for a woman. The thought that being 'Mukta' is not enough or that 'Mukta' needed some tag evoked my rebellious side and an instantly sarcastic reaction. I immediately faked a smile and asked the gentleman, "Would you not give me breakfast if I were just 'Mukta'?"

Being single has been 'life' for me up until now. I do not think of being single as 'different.' I am reminded of the fact that I am single and that, for other people, being single is vastly different. I am reminded of this often by society and my environment. These nudges are sometimes subtle and sometimes loud.

The Escapade

I left home for work when I was all of 23. I never wanted to work in Indore University (where I was already working on a contract) and end up in an arranged marriage. I feared confrontation with family and extended family, and so I moved away from home one evening. My leaving home was quite filmy – in fact, I just quietly applied and took a job in Pune through a newspaper advertisement and then planned to leave home one day. Marriage meant some kind of a chain, a rather sticky something to me at that time. It also meant certain fixed ideas like matchmaking, getting utensils as gifts, adjusting to a man you have never seen before, getting along with his family, and pushing yourself to be someone you may not be. It meant trying to fit into "oh, but this is what everyone does" and I sort of baulked at that.

I never wanted to break away from home this way; there are consequences to all behaviour, and moving away meant much more than leaving a safe haven. It was neither easy on my family nor on me. It meant breaking away from an entire social support system – my parents, grandparents, chatty relatives, childhood friends, nosey neighbours, my teachers, and my hometown. It meant the disapproval of loved ones, their hurt, and many calls urging me to return. I felt like an uprooted young sapling that was looking for another place to grow. I did have some plans, though – I had just registered for my doctorate in marketing to resist marriage.

Looking back, I realise that while I was escaping from what I did not want, I really did not know what I wanted. At 23, I did not have a plan for my life. I just chose to run to a new city because I could not think of a better way to get away. I guess I had chosen a path of disobedience and rebellion to feel free.

I had secured a decent job that gave me a little place to live in Pune, and it catered to most of my physiological requirements. But the emotional uprooting gnawed at me for many years after I left home. My parents shared their anger and helplessness often, and my grandmother wrote me postcards asking me to return. Things cooled down a bit after a couple of years or so. But even then, while I went home to meet my folks every now and then, I never really went home to live.

Growing Up and Fairy Tales

My parents are scientists; they are creative and aesthetic people and have tremendously contributed to my being, besides of course having given me this beautiful life. My father bought us many books; he taught me to ask, "Tell me why?" My mother introduced me to music and art. I grew up with Grimm's and soviet fairy tales, Enid Blyton, Nancy Drew, the Hardy Boys and, eventually, graduated to Mills and Boons, Sidney Sheldon, John Grisham, and the rest. I also had some exposure to Kahlil Gibran, Erich Fromm, Rilke, and J. Krishnamurthy through my father.

All through my adolescent years, I believed in fairy tales, romantic ideas, filmy love, and so on. Well, honestly, I can't say I have stopped even today. Because my ideas of love and romance still peep into my short stories, my poems, and childlike drawings. I can easily say that the real world hasn't taken my dreamy imaginations away from me. Occasionally I still witness the child with rosy glasses in me. I never enjoyed the boredom that arose from the 'routineness' of life. My love for life and curiosity is inherited.

I suspect that my ideas of relating to other people, however, may have stayed a little underdeveloped. I grew up seeing quite a bit of conflict between my parents over small matters such as picking up stuff from where you left it, tasks like folding clothes, cooking, and cleaning, and housemaids. Most of all, I always told myself that conflict was a waste of productive and creative energy. I quickly learnt to adapt to conflict at home, compartmentalise, put disharmony in a box in my head, and do brilliantly at school and college. I may have learnt even from my parents' skirmishes. During this process of growing up and compartmentalising, I also learnt to push sadness away or hide it in a box. I would then bury the box and, if I could, simply never revisit it.

I must also confess that my filmy and rosy glasses led to more than drawings and poems. I made multiple bad choices during my adolescence and even later by imagining fairy-tale endings. I often saw men with my rosy glasses. My romantic ideas of relationships were often seemingly unreal. I have felt immense pain and longing pertaining to my ideas of love. Though I would never complain about any of this, as I had learnt to be by myself. That said, over these years, despite multiple rollercoaster rides, and varied experiences and experiments, life has taught me to look at it with love.

Being Single and Living by Myself

My core value of always having the maximum degrees of freedom and space has been largely responsible for my being single. My belief in immense possibilities and the need to always have choices has only added to it. My being single is also about escaping conflict and not wanting two opinions on every little thing. And this has roots in my childhood where I saw conflict and disharmony over petty matters. Those conflicts seem to have left a very inessential image of marriage in my mind. I am not sure if I even have a distant memory of my parents as a lovey-dovey couple. Lovey-dovey couples were a fairy tale to me, though I believed in them thanks to my love for books and films. To me, loving couples resided in books and movies. Despite what I saw of real couples, I somehow still believed that the prince and the princess actually do live happily ever after. While 'reality' gets thrown at me every now and then when I observe bored couples humiliating each other, or couples in restaurants not even looking at or speaking to each other while eating, even today, I retain a very fairy-tale-like imagination of a couple. This pink idea in my mind, that a romantic couple really exists, refuses to die.

After leaving home when I landed in Pune, where I was living by myself, I felt free of any family or hometown-specific social pressures.

My research work peacefully progressed here; I got a doctorate in 2003 and continued my jobs in multiple corporate firms. My quest for learning and newness stayed unquenchable, and I continued my education and self-development in applied behavioural science. In June of 2017, I started my boutique consulting firm after working with Indian and multinational companies for a little more than 19 years. I also began to pursue painting and writing alongside my profession. I thought I needed all three: colours to relate to and express myself; poetry for touching and expressing my deeper emotions; and work to keep me relevant, purposive, and sane. I also began to do interdisciplinary work to make sense of art, literature, and consulting together, so I did not feel the stark split between creativity and analytics. For instance, I would use visual stimuli, theatre, laboratory method, and literature for my sessions with client organisations. I enjoyed and still enjoy design and interdisciplinary creativity. Being perpetually curious, I never stopped exploring new ways of reaching people. This, too, was my way of integrating my interests and putting myself together. Integrating parts of me and finding and completing self is a slow and a never-ending process. The process is still ongoing – I am perpetually a 'work in progress.'

Being single, I had to do some so-called 'masculine' stuff by myself (picking up a gas cylinder and changing it, for example) or to deal with multiple men to get things done (plumbers, carpenters, security guards, etc.). This needed me to be tougher and harsher than I really am. This was definitely an adaptation to deal with my reality of being by myself. I learnt to use the masculine and feminine sides in me, which, in hindsight, I am certainly grateful for. For instance, I always loved to cook and to feed friends, but I also learnt to drive an SUV with a manual gearbox. I discovered that while I like to collect curios and aesthetic antique jewellery or experiment with new cosmetics, I also love sturdy bikes and large watches like some men do. I got exposed to racing cars while working in the auto sector, predominantly a man's world. I began to enjoy speed and mechanics besides colour and aesthetic. Today, I have multiple men friends with whom I enjoy a conversation about cars, bikes, stock prices, health routines, and many women friends with whom

I enjoy gossip, talking about new cosmetics, fad diets, and their children's school assignments, food preferences, and their own love lives. This switching sides may have helped me to be in touch with the masculine and the feminine within me and feel complete.

Socially, am I alone? The answer to that is a 'yes' and a 'no.' I have been in love. I have had relationships with men. I do not live with a partner. I have experienced the beauty of a romantic relationship. I love being in a relationship, but I do not yearn to be in one always. Do I want to be in the socially acceptable relationship that they call marriage? Well, I am not averse to it, but it is not a precondition to my happiness. Relating to people does make me happy, but it also takes away my happiness sometimes.

I crave 'aloneness' after interactions with groups, systems, friends, relatives, and people of all kinds. I cherish that space within me – 'being alone' is indeed an important space. Philosophically speaking, I believe deeply and thoroughly in my 'aloneness' and the 'aloneness' of each one of us. And I don't mean lonely by 'alone'. Since I have lived alone for quite some time, relating to self has been the kind of relating I have predominantly focused on. I have learnt to love myself probably because I thought no one loved me in my difficult moments. Or at least not in the way I wanted to be loved and supported. Over a period of time, I gradually began to feel that I am enough for myself. I do not deny that there are times when I look for approval, recognition, and affection from my primary system, from my loved ones and friends in particular and society in general. But somehow, I do not imagine myself looking for approval, recognition, love, security, and affection from that one man who one would socially call a husband, a partner, or a lover. I am not averse to receiving all this from that one man, but I wouldn't depend on it – possibly because I do not trust that I shall steadily receive all this from him. If I look back, being single has not so much been a matter of choice for me: I haven't come across that someone with unconditional positive regard for me, whom I could love and cherish.

When I look back, I feel that I may have overcompensated for my lack of feeling loved and related to (during my earlier life) by focusing a lot more on my achievements – both material and intellectual. Maybe all I really wanted was some freedom to be my own person. I sometimes wonder if such simple stuff is too much to ask for. When I pushed my limits at work, I did not find time for sadness and confusion. Honing my skills and learning also helped me. There have been times when I may have kept very busy just to push away some sadness that came from being misunderstood by the people I loved the most – my family, some friends, and even some men I respected and cared for.

Comparisons

I have often wondered if I miss something in my life – and the answer to that one is interestingly very different at a superficial than at a deeper level. At a certain level, I have experienced a sense of insecurity (socially); often when I get couple invites or wedding invites, I do feel the need to have someone to call my own to go along with. But at a deeper level, I understand that we do not own anyone or anything, and then I don't feel that need anymore. Do I feel insecure about being taken care of at times? Yes, I do. But when I often see married men and women who feel even more insecure than I have ever felt, I feel better for myself. Besides, having friends to chat with about multiple facets of life, about my many highs and lows, bright and dull moments, has been very helpful. Over a period of time, I have learnt that one's sense of security is not out there with someone else. The sense of grounded-ness and anchoring has to come from deep within oneself. My sense of security comes from my own strength, my love for self, and the power of my will – these, I believe, are my most valued assets.

Having read a bit of anthropology, I understand that human beings are naturally polygamous. I have also seen some marriages rather closely. I have dear friends who have confided in me – whispered to me about the boredom in their marriages, their lingering sense of dissatisfaction from the arrangement, and their feeling of being stuck in it. I have seen some friends struggling with infidelity (emotional infidelity being the most common) and their own restrictive role boundaries. I have seen up close the inability of married men and women to move out of their self-created comfort zones, and many conflicts arising from this. To me, such a situation could feel like a prison, like revolving in an incessant loop – and even imagining this is very scary for me. My experience of being single within myself has been joyful and liberating. I must say that I love my freedom a whole lot. I have felt freer in comparison to many of my friends. I feel relieved for myself, particularly when I see a friend giving lengthy explanations to their spouse about where they have been or what they are up to. By sheer contrast, when I am able to spend my time with whoever in whatever fashion I want to, I suddenly feel fortunate. I have felt loved by friends for being the free spirit that they call me. Some of them even feel inspired by my being – and some of them secretly envy me for my freedom. I have always taken pride in being my own person.

To balance my perspective, I have also come across some happy couples with well-brought-up children. But those couples would admit that their marriages were built and sustained with effort. Also, if one observed them closely, the sense of space and individuality is often compromised for both. Besides, in these successful and happy marriages, if one were to look at all the data points carefully, nevertheless one partner looked professionally more successful than the other. And often enough, the more successful partner happened to be the man (who sometimes is even ungrateful for what the other has done or forgone). So, while it is difficult to say that marriages might prevent women from being professionally successful, the whole idea of marriage has never felt so convincingly awesome to me. Having said all this, I don't shut out those possibilities, and I haven't ever given up on relating, romance, sex, love, care, and companionship. If a loving companionship happens for me, that would be another lovely adventure. While I seek this adventure from within, I don't depend on it for my happiness, security, or satisfaction.

Exclusions and Inclusions

I have had moments when my singlehood has been pointed out as different and abnormal by systems, even by friends and by my loved ones. I have seen those views in perspective and have never felt intimidated or limited by them.

Yes, I have had arguments, sometimes heated ones with my family – my mother in particular. I have felt sad and misunderstood at times, and often, I have found myself standing alone in such conversations. I have had candid chats and debates with my friends on the subject, and they have been more understanding of my stance. But I must say that unconditional acceptance hasn't come by very often. I have felt anger – when I was linked romantically and sexually to any man who gave me a ride on his bike, or any man who helped me get something done or was seen having a cup of coffee with me a few times. I have heard gossip about me – "Oh! Is she a lesbian?" "Oh! She is moody and unpredictable, maybe she is sex deprived." "Oh! She is pretty and educated and all that a woman wants to be, so why can't she find a nice guy?" I have been asked questions like "Don't you feel like having sex?" "How do you satisfy your urges?" I have been asked out by several men who thought that being single meant I am available (and worse still, available *to them*). My friends have set me up with some men I found totally unacceptable, and there are times when I have felt betrayed.

Dealing with Feelings

Feelings have been a mixed bag for me. Being a sensitive person, I have felt my feelings very intensely. I have also learnt to accept them. My feelings peep into my poems and paintings. My moments of missing a sense of belongingness show up in my poetry.

Creativity in its various forms gives me joy. New experiences through travel, painting, observing nature carefully, and writing about life and love give me joy. I appreciate art, experiment with food, act, sing, dance, and appreciate beauty in its various forms. Appreciation of my painting by a connoisseur or the way a viewer interprets it and the impact it has on them give me joy. I believe that much of my art and words are a sublimation of my desires, even longings – I can say my books and paintings are tangible manifestations of how I have felt life and my bag of experiences. My creative energy probably is the energy that I would have otherwise spent building a family, raising children, and keeping up with and relating to many derived relationships that automatically come with a marriage. I guess my energy gets utilised and distributed over multiple life-giving activities and experiences in the absence of marriage and kids. If I were in a marriage or a relationship, would I have been as productive and creative? Maybe yes, if I had a cool guy around, but maybe not – I can't say. They say we create to complete something in us or even to release something hidden within. I relate to both when creativity manifests itself through me.

Relating to others, making new friends, cooking, and feeding friends and loved ones give me joy. I enjoy being loved truly; I enjoy candour in relationships. Taking care of my health, staying fit, and exercising give me joy. Aesthetic pursuits like doing up my house, tending to my little plants, and hedonistic pursuits like massages and shopping for exquisite stuff give me joy. Reading gives me joy, particularly philosophy, fiction, old classics, and sometimes even absurd stuff. The way Haruki Murakami describes love, or Kahlil Gibran's philosophy of relating, or Rilke's passion as he writes his *Letters to a Young Poet*, these have all deeply inspired my ways, my writing, and my life. In moments of feeling lonely in my decisions, unsure, or in dealing with feeling rejected sometimes, I have found succour in the works of Dr. Clarissa Pinkola Estes. Her book *Women Who Run with the Wolves* has impacted me deeply. *The Little Prince* by Saint-Exupéry, *The Prophet* by Kahlil Gibran, and Oscar Wilde's *The Portrait of Dorian Gray* come to mind often – I have gone back and read them multiple times. Carl Jung's writing and lectures have also helped me delve deeper into myself. At work, I enjoy facilitation – helping someone sort themselves, ease some pain, or helping someone discover a new realm or a fresh perspective gives me joy. I enjoy learning and exploring – achievements, academic or otherwise, my productivity, whether it is setting up a new business or writing the last line of a poem.

Dilemmas and Pain

I have my own dilemmas. The very first one is whether to own up to some sense of regret for being single or stay deeply convinced that I have no regrets. Regrets have always been a dangerous area for me to explore because they could flood me with negativity and sadness. But whenever I have reflected on regrets or tried to explore them, luckily, I don't find very much there. I do struggle with what kind of relationships to have with a man. Do I surrender myself and unconditionally give in a relationship? How do I keep a self-preservative balance? How do I manage the boundaries of relationships in a way that gives me the space I need and meets the expectations of the other? Then there are also those dilemmas of balancing between sensitivity to self and sensitivity to the other. At a deeper level, I see this as an unresolved cold war between the head and the heart.

As a woman (and not necessarily because I am single), I already struggle to balance social acceptability and competence accolades. For example, I have heard people saying *"Yar, Khadoos hai, magar kaam bohot acha karti hai"* [she is rude but she does a great job at work]. Then there are the blurry lines between *"Pyaari hai"* [she is cute] and *"Hot hai yar"* [she is hot], so there is a dilemma of managing my attractiveness as a woman alongside my competence. There is a dilemma of being feminine and vulnerable besides the anxiety of feeling abused/invaded when people respond to that. There are questions like "am I inviting a problem by just being who I am?" that often come to mind. I felt the pain of being looked upon as 'available' because I am single, gossiped about, and even unwanted by men (even a couple of women). I have felt pained when married women looked at me with suspicious eyes – as if they were sure that I would take their spouses away from them.

Being an attractive single woman is not easy. Even one's primary system often emotively makes you feel alienated. When I share my concern, I have often been told that "if you naturally emit sexuality, you cannot control whether a bull gets attracted to it or a bee gets attracted to it. You have got to learn to manage that." At work, I have faced the dilemma of how to confront soft misogyny. Whether to use fight or flight – whether to deflect misogyny, whether to use humour or confrontation. Dilemmas of what filters to apply and how to filter and consciously choose sunlight without the ultraviolet – and how do I selectively bring parts of myself in relationships? I still struggle to sort some of this today.

I do understand that some of my longings come from imaginations of love and romance. Potential men or the men I like often do not fit into my fairy tales. But over the years, I have learnt that love and romance have multiple ways of being expressed. And that I must stop penalising men for not coming up to my (seemingly high) standards that require the other to consistently see me for who I am and have unconditional positive regard for me as I would have for them. My standards are crafted by me, and I am proud of them. But now that I have grown up, I also understand that a man's love could look quite different from my imagination of love.

Pain and suffering have taught me some acceptance. My pain has always made me curious – I have learnt a lot from pain. With my experiences, I have come to see relating somewhat differently and rather expansively. It also helps me feel detached and involved at the same time. Being a single woman, I have been learning about 'passionately creating' and then 'giving away,' and I have felt this same attachment and detachment in my relationships as well – I loved deeply when I loved, and let go when it was time. My mother says to me, "you haven't felt what being a mother feels like and that too is about creating passionately and then giving away." I agree with her, but maybe we are meant to create and give away different things while we are around. My pains and dilemmas have propelled a strangely spiritual part in me that is blurry right now, but I can say that I am beginning to notice it.

Needs and Compartments

I need an infrastructure for getting things done – apps like UrbanClap, Uber, Ola, Bill Pay, Alexa, Big Basket, and Swiggy – the more the merrier for me! Sometimes I wish I had a perfect artificial-intelligence robot that could help around the house. And for sure I need some people to help, such as a housekeeper, a security guard, a driver, some shops with home delivery, and a laundry with home delivery. But as well as physical conveniences, I also need a psychological infrastructure – people who understand me, some compartmentalised relationships to meet my companionship needs, thought partnership, my need for recreation, for my 'meaning of life' conversations, sex and love, and a way of managing all of this. These specific articulated needs seem like compartments when you look at them very clinically, but I do need these boxes because I believe different people fit in separate boxes, and it may be convenient (and borderline selfish) most of the time. If I think of a companion, I would like to be with someone who shares my interests, loves life, and has an interesting world view. I must say that I also have an acceptance for these compartments in the other person. Well, I have not found someone who even appreciates these boxes and compartments in me.

Currently, I share my interests, gifts, and other parts of me with people I place in separate boxes in my heart and mind. In a companion, of course, I seek someone with whom I can share most parts of me – for instance, if I have had a bad day at work, I would like to share it with him and expect him to listen empathetically; or if I had just visited Cappadocia I would love to share my experience of the love valley with him, and I would want him to share my enthusiasm. I would like him to understand that I need a hug without my saying it or understand almost automatically that I am feeling lonely in a decision-making process when I am feeling that way. I would like him to understand that I hate the math of a GST calculation or my obsessive need for cleanliness, aesthetics and all the little stuff, and I would want him to be OK with it. And now, I would love to be with someone who understands the woman inside my seemingly hardened exterior – an exterior that is hardened by doing stuff all by myself and being strong all the time. I would do the same for someone I chose to be with and love. In the absence of such a companion, my psychological infrastructure could include as many people as there are boxes and interests. My expectation from society is that of understanding these compartments. I expect people to understand that the person I discuss tennis with may not be the person I would like to make love to under the stars.

A bit of what I am about to say might sound unfair, but I will attempt to explain it. While I want to be accepted as I am and as a whole, I want to engage with different parts of people. While I understand that people are a package, there are many parts of them I may not want to engage with. For example, the classic dilemma I often face is of engaging intellectually with a man who wants me romantically or sexually. When I was younger, this kind of engagement ended in my feeling conflict and disgust. With some maturity kicking in, I have stopped getting upset about such differences in expectations. I have begun to understand this phenomenon by looking at it both objectively and empathetically. But even now, sometimes, when I want to discuss and engage with people or those parts of them, they may see me as selfish. It is not as if I am unwilling to accept a person as a whole person. I do accept many of my dear friends fully and unconditionally, but I choose not to engage with some parts of them that intrude on my sacred spaces.

What all this means practically is that I spend some of my energy managing boundaries. Managing boundaries in line with expectations in a relationship on both sides requires constant work. As a single woman, I am constantly managing boundaries with multiple men – and this process saps energy that could be creatively utilised elsewhere.

Society and Me

I would like to share my gifts with society. I would like to realise my potential. Whether through commercial activity, vocational activity, or altruism – the impact is important to me. I believe I am here on this earth for something more important than just living and wading through. I am here for something productive, creative, and facilitative – all three and maybe more. I would like to give my best version to society. I perpetually consider myself as a 'work in progress.' The idea is to chisel and finish and polish myself like a piece of art (I don't mean this in a narcissistic way). I wish to be able to give my best shot at living in this world.

I want to experience the world, process it, interpret it, and give out something unique that hasn't been offered to the world before – I want to give something that Mukta created or built or facilitated or made, and then leave it for this world when I leave. Those possibilities really excite me.

I would like society to treat me with respect and understanding. And also, take note of my individual identity – and love and respect me for the person inside this body of a woman and what I joyfully bring to this world. I would want people to see me, the whole person and not a stereotype such as 'single woman,' 'consultant,' 'poet,' 'artist,' or 'actor.'

A Happy Farm – My Fairy Tale about Dying

I am unsure about being single forever. But even if I stay single, given who I am, I might have many friends around. Companionship, if that happens, would be very welcome. Given how I live for the day and the moment, I honestly don't mind conking off before actually growing old. I don't have any fixed plans for my old age.

So, what does being 60 mean to me as a single woman? I am guessing that I am rather playful about my old age. I haven't thought this through carefully, but I do have a fairy tale about it. I imagine my old age would be lived in a community of friends who have a great sense of humour – on a farm with multiple houses and a common food place, a kind of sanctuary where everyone lives the way they want, relate in the way they want, and are free to choose and wish – a place full of possibilities. This farm would be happy and peaceful. I am rather optimistic about old age, and I am often told that I should be a little more realistic, in a 'hope for the best and prepare for the worst' kind of way. Growth – intellectual, emotive or spiritual – would mean losing parts of me, and finally, it would even mean decomposing to be a different combination of atoms again. The poet in me possibly believes that moving on from home, workplaces, lovers, or life could just be the same thing. I wish to become a verse or a song, as my breath becomes air.

A Note to Other Single Women

I understand that there is no one right way to live, no magic formula; but I would like to share what has helped me in my journey up until now. I am conscious of the chat that I have with myself. The good quality of self-talk has tremendously helped me stay happy.

I consciously do not let myself be pressured into desperately trying to be like someone else, regarding my marital status. I have never seen singlehood as abnormal. I believe that I am unique, I have come with a purpose, and hence I don't see a reason to comply with institutions just for the sake of it or just to feel secure in society. I have not made sub-optimal decisions to be in relationships or marriage just because someone would call me single, point a finger at me, or question my identity, bereft of a man. I am convinced that this finger-pointing could happen irrespective of whether you are single or not, and not getting pressured to do something my heart and mind does not agree with has been helpful.

I have learnt that empathy is vital and that it brings me closer to people. Empathy allows us to function as more than just self-obsessed individuals.

Next, being comfortable with the insecurities arising out of small stuff like "Now that I am going to work and the new maid has to work alone, will she be careful about my expensive China or ceramic curios while I am away?" or "Will the security guard safely keep the packet received from Amazon while I am away?", and much larger stuff like "What will I do alone in my old age and who will look after me when I am sick?" Well, reducing the volume of negative self-talk has helped me tremendously.

I have looked carefully at the messages I grew up with and even my values, and have held them up and asked – are these working for me in my current context? Does my lifestyle make me feel satisfied and peaceful in the here and now? I believe that if I am not happy and peaceful myself, I shall never be able to create an environment of happiness, love, and peace. And hence I have learnt that being sensitive to self is a priority – and not simply that, but doing it without feeling selfish or guilty about it.

I have learnt that meaning and purpose are the key, and structures and interdependencies are what we build; roles are clothes that we wear. But understanding and knowing the person without those roles is crucial.

Self-love and self-acceptance have been immensely helpful in my journey. Periodically reflecting to check the health of my self-esteem and what it brings with it have helped me. I have learnt from multiple experiences and haven't ever stopped learning. Pulling myself out of my comfort zone and looking at multiple perspectives has been a climb for me, but it has been worth the effort. Working on self, thinking, and reflecting deeply on who I am, the meaning that I give to myself, my relationships and my expectations from myself and society have been immensely helpful.

It has always helped me to focus on my physical fitness, diet, and rest. I may not be extraordinarily strong, but I am usually fit for a ten-kilometre run. I ensure that I exercise, eat, and sleep well to be able to stay upbeat. I love life and keep a positive, happy disposition.

I can say I consciously programme my nerves to remain happy, despite the odds. And then it becomes a habit.

Awareness (practising it at the Indian Society of Applied Behavioural Science), living in the here and now, recognising that I change over time (we all do), and responding to stimuli in a way that helps, builds, and shapes life have helped me tremendously. To me, in essence, being single has been about embracing a journey of self-discovery, learning, and understanding that the "The purpose of life is to find your gift and the meaning of life is to give it away."

All in All

I see my life as an adventure – with twists, turns, surprises. Life has surprised me enough times to keep that faith alive. Singlehood and adventure somehow go hand in hand. The last 20 years of my life have been filled with adventure, travel, meeting people, falling in love with people and countries, a lot of hard work, unbelievably diverse experiences, and no regrets at all. Life to me is about experiencing and being grateful for those experiences.

While we were playfully chatting over a cup of coffee, I once said to an old friend, "I love myself, and I love my life." And he asked me, "Mukta, if you got one more chance at life would you like to be born as this same Mukta again?" I found the question remarkably interesting, and without blinking an eyelid, I spontaneously said "Oh, most definitely yes! I would love to be born and to live as this Mukta once again. And I think I shall try some different things in this new life you're giving me a chance at. And I shall write a new story about a new set of experiences even then. And I am sure that even my new story will be as interesting and lovable as this one."

*****

Single Women Lives: Significant Themes and Patterns

Uma Jain

The uniqueness, the commonalities, and the richness of these stories will be seen and experienced by the readers in each individual journey. In this chapter, I have culled from the data the major themes, patterns, commonalities, and the main learnings from these writings on the life journeys of single women. I believe this analysis will answer some of the repetitive questions about single women's lives for people curious about them and those in the process of decision-making about their own lives. I also hope that it will help construct a more real and dignifying narrative about single women's lives rather than operating on unreal and *undignifying* assumptions and stories.

The themes that I talk about in this chapter are the significant ones; they appear and re-appear in the different chapters above (though not necessarily in all), as well as in what I have often heard in my conversations with other single women who are not part of this book. Many of these are common across borders, while I also mention some differences between Indian and Western women.

1. Is Being Single a Choice and/or a One-time Decision?

One of the common questions asked of single women is "Why did you choose to remain single?' – particularly if the woman has never been married, as there are many unspoken assumptions in people's minds about unmarried women. For the women of a seemingly marriageable age who become single again after a marriage, there is a similar question that may be asked less often. The journeys in this book, as well as many other stories that I have listened to, help build some hypotheses to answer this question.

In the lives of single women, there are different paths which have taken them to singlehood. Being single is often not a clear one-time decision to start with, as is often imagined. The dominant social norms seem so deep-rooted that most women in this book saw the possibility of making a family life, a heterosexual companionship, love and physical intimacy to be preferably sought (or even only to be acceptable) in a long-term marriage relationship (or at least in one intended to be so).

For most of the women, a clarity of values emerged as they moved along and experimented with various options. They went through a process of exploring the choices that social systems offered them, and the marriage possibilities which came their way. It was difficult to find partners who would allow them the experience of being whole, and the freedom to work, love, and grow. In that process, they evolved their sense of clarity about what they wanted, as well as discovered ways of living life meaningfully without marriage. Singlehood was an outcome of their deep-rooted values and priorities for which they had experienced rejections from men and social systems. They came to believe that the patriarchal social system would not give them the desired opening in their life.

For some, clarity emerged only after disappointing, painful marriages conflicting with what they stood for, and which they chose to leave. Sometimes married life was ended by an unfortunate event such as the death of a spouse. However, staying single after that has been a choice.

Therefore, being single has been an emerging, evolving choice but not in the sense of a one-time decision, forever. It is often an eventual result of a series of decisions taken over a long period of time and resulting from the discovery and pursuit of the women's values in personal, social, and professional spheres. However, underlying the whole process was often a stand that marriage would not be the primary goal of life. The women did not want to be in a wedded partnership at the cost of their other significant personal values. This was a departure from the prevailing social norms and pattern of marriage as a must.

2. The 'Why' of Being Single: A Quiet Feminism

There are some positive or driving forces which make women move towards being single as an attractive option and there are some negative or dampening forces which make them want to keep away from marriage. Both seem to go together, are interconnected and lead to the choice.

Some of the forces at the root of the decision to remain single for several women include the desire for freedom, learning, achievement, personal growth, being true to themselves, self-actualisation, spiritual evolution, adventure, love for travelling, and contribution to profession or society. Observing married women not experiencing the freedom to fulfil some of these desires became a force to not enter into marriage and instead to choose a single life for pursuing and fulfilling these.

The process of arranging marriages (for some Indian women) and a lack of visible examples of happy and meaningful marriages made some women want to stay away from matrimony. For some, experiences of deceit and betrayal by men in relationships or sexual abuse in childhood or marriage led to cynicism and distrust towards men. These are some of the forces which have made women stay away from marriage or become single after marriage.

In a nutshell, choosing to remain single is a different form of feminism – not to keep fighting for equality in a patriarchal setup or taking up legal battles for sexual harassment or domestic abuse – but it is a quiet decision. It means not succumbing to an exploitative system where either the entry itself or continuing meant succumbing to inequality, injustice, exploitation, or a sense of indignity. Some examples of this include dowry requirements prior to a marriage; being expected to take on the primary burden of home responsibilities after marriage, as pre-decided by others; setting the limits of one's career to meet family needs; and having to be dependent on one's husband, even to use income the woman had herself earned. It is an act of taking charge of their life when they do not find anyone by their side.

Viewed from another perspective, all of these pressures have been felt by many other women who nevertheless did not remain single. While many causes have provided the impetus to be single, there is also some element of destiny. These women walked this path perhaps because it was their work in this world, in this lifetime, to experience, understand, and articulate the processes of being single on behalf of society.

3. Models of Living

There are different models of living a single life emerging, including: adopting a child as a single parent to create a family of one's own; creating a psychological family amongst friends and professional colleagues but living alone; living with parental family with or without a child; and many others. Several single women chose to leave their homes and some even left the cities where they had lived with their parental families, to pursue their passions and goals. They lived alone, in hostels or in a spiritual ashram, whether having never married or after leaving a marriage. Some continue to live with their parental families or later go back to them. Some live with their children – their own, their ex-husband's, or adopted. However, even adopting a child for a single woman is not an easy process, both from legal and other requirements, and society's reactions.

Some cultural differences impact single women's lives in terms of what they do, but not how they feel. For example, in some of the writings, the lives of Western women, whether unmarried or after a divorce, seem to show much more dating and relationships with men than those of Indian women. But the experience of relationships seems similar.

4. Questioning Patriarchal Traditions, Norms, and Prescriptions

A sense of rebellion towards the patriarchal system is a prevalent theme in single women journeys. For example, in India this can be provoked by the dowry and the process of arranging marriages, or the widely prevalent concepts of the man–woman relationship and roles, with the associated expectations from women. The single women did not want their lives defined solely by social norms or their spouses. They want a say in making them. They want choices. Some of them attempted to adapt to the patriarchal system, but could not continue to do so because, for them, independence, love for truth, and freedom were deeply held values.

Social pressure placed on women to marry is often based on certain assumptions about how life should be and what makes it safer, stable, and happy. Single women do not see safety and stability as the goals of life. They questioned such ideas as a reason to marry. They also do not see marriage as a necessary criterion for getting respect and acceptance, even if often it is so. Reading feminist writings or associating with people with similar values further strengthened their inclinations.

5. Society in Transition: Contradictory Messages

Single women in this book tend to be achievers. Achievement was often encouraged or even expected by the family in younger life, and this attitude towards achievement in terms of getting better grades than others and so on was cultivated in the process of growing up. At the same time, there was also a concern in some parents that if their daughters pursued higher professional studies beyond a point, it would become difficult to find a husband more qualified than their daughter, who would also be over-age for marriage. Educational achievements, however, were not valued in the process of finding a partner or during married life. Contradictions within family messages and a sense of non-acceptance of the growing, evolving person is evident in many writings.

It seems that parents often adopted what was then emerging as the norm regarding the education of their daughters without a clear understanding of what being educated would entail. They did not envision the other changes it would bring with it. Many parents saw education as a means to find a good match and make the daughter capable to earn, but not to be so professional as to make work a priority rather than homemaking. In terms of gender images, stereotypes, and roles, society remained far behind the economic progress. Traditionally masculine qualities were valued and nurtured significantly in the growing-up years of several women. Then, as they matured, they were suddenly expected to demonstrate traditionally defined feminine attitudes and standards which had not been cultivated up to that point. It seems that the age-old patriarchal script was expected to be followed and lived irrespective women's education.

Therefore, as vividly described by some of the women in their journeys, it seems that many single women belong to a section of society that at one level has adopted the social change regarding daughters, in terms of opportunities for education and working outside the home. However, consciously or unconsciously, a woman's role and life are still seen from a traditional perspective. The responsibility of managing their own wishes and aspirations in this context thus falls upon the women themselves. Some chose to work to meet all the expectations and kept adjusting and negotiating within the system of marriage, while these single women questioned them.

Interestingly, both in Western and Indian societies, it seems that patriarchal expectations from women do exist. In Indian women's journeys, they are expressed directly, even as parental expectation while growing up, socialising both men and women in patriarchy. In Western women's journeys, these expectations appear as the more subtle, unconscious, internalised image of a woman's role amongst both women and men. Hence, in Western countries, the degree of social change may be more visible and apparent, but patriarchal values and expectations about women's roles nevertheless continue and can be a factor in a woman's being single.

6. Feelings of Being Different and Othered

Many of the single women's values and passions – freedom, self-expression, self-actualisation, experiencing their wholeness, a commitment to professional contribution, and so on – do not fall into the prevalent norms of society. They break the stereotype of a soft-spoken, nurturing, accommodating woman who puts others' needs before her own. Hence, single women tend to carry a sense of being different, separate, away from the crowd or norm that is may be inborn and/or cultivated by early circumstances.

Several women talk about having role models different from their own mothers. They do not see as their ideal model a woman who falls comfortably (or uncomfortably but quietly) into the social mould of expectations and makes peace with them. Their models are special people – women or men who stood out, made a mark in the world, and were different from the crowd.

Single women also carry a feeling of being othered by people and society due to their different lifestyle and values in life. Being othered seems to be a common thread running through several stories.

7. The Urge to Build Self-esteem and Develop Self

One theme emerging for several women in this book is that of an underlying sense of worthlessness and not valuing their own self. This seems to have been inculcated consciously or unconsciously due to being discriminated against, or even unwanted, as a girl child. This can occur as a result of being compared to male siblings, or being rejected as a girl due to colour or because one's personality differs from the stereotypical expectations of a girl child, for example. In Indian women's journeys, this theme appears more directly, stated as being connected to being a woman, but it is also quite prevalent in Western women's journeys, though enacted in a different form. At one level, we could say that this would be likely to emerge as a theme even if we studied the lives of women in general. What makes these women different and leads to the choice or outcome of being single? It is their awareness of these discriminatory processes and often a sense of rebellion against them. They also have a deep-rooted urge to emerge out of this into a life of freedom, living their own values and developing a sense of self-worth, as well as being of value to others and society. It has often led to being professionally competent, expressive, and standing up for their values.

An urge for self-actualisation and a desire for self-respect seem to occur as both the causes of singlehood as well as the outcomes thereof. Self-development and self-realisation are the goals of many; some seek these through the path of behavioural science and others through the Indian Vedic tradition. Some have had their own gradual discovery process of finding themselves through life experiences, introspection, reading, and so on.

8. Relationships with Men: Struggle with Strengths and Vulnerabilities

Most of the women in this book talk about their desire to be accepted in their wholeness by their partner – the different aspects of themselves, particularly the strength that they have and build further over time and their vulnerability. They would like to be accepted, appreciated, and valued for all of these rather than being fixed or labelled as either strong or emotional, or being expected to behave in a certain consistent style. It seems that the men in their experience, who are drawn to their strength, are not comfortable with their vulnerability when it shows up, and walk away or the relationship withers. For some women, this resulted in their never entering marriage, while the married ones ended the marriage. Over a period of time, it seems to become a cycle which further enhances the strength with which the women deal with their vulnerability and hide it, which in turn keeps away those men who are not comfortable with strength.

Women are also looking for an open and complete relationship with their partners which seems to be impossible in their experience. They find men also bound in traditional masculine roles and not comfortable sharing their vulnerability. Women seem to want a competent, open, as well as understanding person as partner – a combination of masculine and feminine qualities, which they often do not find. They have the urge to be seen, heard, and loved, as well as respected for who they are as a person, which they do not experience in relationship with men. Women are longing for love, partnership, authentic sharing, and acceptance of their whole emerging being in marriage, not just sex, protection, or a role-based relationship. They find themselves chasing a mirage.

9. Singlehood and Sexuality

There is much, somewhat uncanny, curiosity about the sex life of single women. Also, there are imaginations ranging from single women being available, asexual, or promiscuous, conveniently assuming or implying that all married people have 'normal' sexual lives. However, sexuality does not come out as a central or even significant theme in the writings of most women in this book. Many Indian women largely did not write on this aspect. Some women, not all of whom wrote for this book, have shared this aspect with me in personal conversations. Western women have also chosen not to talk about it at length, except for one woman. A few writings have brought out some data on dating and sex. Hence, my understanding of this theme is based on data as well as an absence of data in the stories and my personal dialogues.

The women writing about their journeys did not speak to the status of their sexual orientation. In my personal conversations with women not a part of this book, there were no references to experiences of same-sex relationships. This could be due to the nature of my circle of acquaintances and friends or the comparative unwillingness to be open about such relationships.

In some women's lives, the relationships with men were also sexual. However, they ended soon due to the absence of certain aspects such as love, partnership, mutual sharing, and respect. This left the women feeling disappointed and unfulfilled. Some women desired the relationship to be potentially sexual, but it ended as it progressively came to their awareness that essential aspects of the relationship were missing. Some wanted a sexual relationship only in matrimony. When the man they dated promised marriage directly or indirectly, but which was not in sight, the woman felt cheated. Some single women have had sexual relationships without an intention or promise to marry. They found these relationships dissatisfying and meaningless due to the absence of feeling accepted as a whole person and ended them. Some have used other methods to meet their physical needs independent of men.

Hence, on the whole, for most single women, sex is not an indispensable need or a central focus. They have found a focus and substitute in their passion for work, building several close warm and loving relationships, and spirituality. They have learnt to live with this part missing from their lives with less difficulty than the absence of a continuing partnership and companionship. In some cases, platonic loving relationships with men have fulfilled this need.

There may or may not be more to it. However, I believe we also do not know enough about this aspect of the lives even of people who fit into the dominant narratives of society.

10. Prevalent Society Narratives about Single Women

The stories in this book bring out the following repetitive images, assumptions, and narratives about single women which get conveyed directly or indirectly.

a) A single woman is a lonely, deprived person hankering for relationships with men and hence a potential threat to marriages. Married women tend to be suspicious if a single woman relates to their husband as a colleague and/or a friend. Hence, single women often do not get invited to some social gatherings. A number of writers have experienced this and shared it in their journey. This leads to distancing in relationships – from men colleagues and friends, new social acquaintances, and even their erstwhile women and men friends, leading to further isolation.

a) It has also been mentioned by several writers that men tend to assume that a single woman is available for a sexual relationship when they want, as she is needy anyway. The use of such labels for single women as 'footloose and fancy free' and 'single, ready to mingle' has also been mentioned in the journeys. Men assuming their availability and proposing sex or physical relationships, even offering to 'satisfy their needs' or 'oblige in all forms,' has also been mentioned.

Unwelcome advances by men to single women make it difficult for single women to retain social contacts, even professionally, which impacts their careers in the long run.

b) Another narrative built up in a different social context by some people often exists side by side with the prevailing narrative of the deprived, lonely, and available single woman. This view imagines the single woman as a very strong, self-sufficient woman, not interested, and hence not requiring inclusion, in social spaces. These narratives feed on each other, enhancing the sense of isolation.

c) A single woman has time on her hands, not having much to do, and hence can be expected to serve when needed. This has come out in a number of stories in the book, as well as conversations: people in the family assuming that they can be called upon at any time as the engagements they make – whether connected to professional work, a vacation or outing, or anything else – are not essential or unchangeable, while married people's engagements are more important.

How this plays out in professional life is that some supervisors and colleagues in organisations assume that a single woman does not have any responsibilities at home and therefore may be called upon to work overtime on weekdays and weekends. At the same time, if she succeeds due to her hard work and competence, there are comments about inappropriate relationships with bosses and so forth, or they are seen as making things difficult for others since the single woman 'has no other responsibility.'

d) There is a prevalent notion that since a single woman does not have children, she does not need much money or even a share in the property of her parents. When my father passed away, my own dear brother, with all his good thinking and intentions, said the following to me: "I believe you would not need any share in the property of our father since you do not have children." There seems to be a belief that a single person does not need to, should not, or even cannot enjoy various things in life that families enjoy, despite the single person being able to afford them and despite these things not being connected to married life. This could also mean indirectly taking advantage of their single status, assuming that a single woman does not need comfort (not even a spacious apartment) or luxuries, irrespective of her own financial status. Or, perhaps viewing money as to be accumulated to leave for children, deciding that she need not or does not deserve to own much wealth since she does not have children. This seems particularly illogical: people with children and family will probably have the latter to help, if and when needed, while a single woman will often need to rely on her own resources. This makes me believe that such beliefs and assumptions are unconscious.

e) Since the single woman has no husband and children (this is the assumption, but it is also reality for most of them), it is sometimes even felt that maybe she does not even need to eat complete meals. She does not deserve a cook or much household help. "Why do you need to cook? You can eat some bread and butter," was actually said to me by some of my neighbours, who found me hiring help. Other women have shared similar experiences. These reactions could also be coming from an unconscious envy.

11. Unwelcome and *Undignifying* Social Reactions

Single women journeys bring out a sense of being singled out in social circles in unwelcome and unpleasant ways. There are some themes that come up in several stories.

Some people demonstrate curiosity about our writers' personal and sexual lives, interest in the reasons for their being single, and presumptions about their possible fears and loneliness through unsolicited questions and statements, conveying subtle pity, suggestions, advice on how to find a partner, or even proposals. Married women also make statements about the imagined freedom and lack of responsibility in the life of a single woman, perhaps from envy or jealousy.

Such social reactions happen even in cases of divorce and widowhood, and not only with unmarried women. Women who are widowed or divorced are subjected to expressions of pity, conveying various norms, expectations, judgements, and suchlike not conducive to self-respect and adding to their feelings of being misunderstood, pain, and isolation.

Various kinds of social responses and questions lead to a situation in which a single woman feels obliged to explain her singlehood and lifestyle, whether she wants to or not.

12. Manipulative and Exploitative Encounters with Men

Another theme emerging, particularly in Indian stories, is that of (what turn out to be) inauthentic or manipulative attempts by men to relate to, or to use the vulnerability of, single women. Several women have narrated in their journey that some of the men they related to were either dishonest or uncommitted in the relationship. It is also a possibility that competent, independent women are found attractive by some men who do not visualise them as possible spouses. They want to relate to them but not make a commitment. This is not to indicate that all men are this way, but that there are enough such people that several of the single women here have encountered them, some repeatedly.

When some of the women have attempted to find a partner, they have encountered dishonest, deceitful men approaching them through marital and dating websites, some of whom are not even single but married, systematically working to take advantage of the women's vulnerability and even to use them financially. Even formerly married women, trying to find a partner after divorce or losing their spouse to death, found themselves being cheated.

In the Western stories, interestingly, women talk about their search for relationships with men and how they ended up not finding what they were looking for. While the relationships are not always built with the perceived or stated promise of marriage, women want more out of relationships than what they experience. Hence, their disappointment and sense of being let down in relationships are similar to those of Indian women. In some of the Western stories, the man depended on the financial resources of the woman.

13. What Do Single Women Feel Good About?

Single women feel good about the freedom, the work, the contribution they are able to make, and the ability to take decisions about their own lives. Several of them talk about a rich life of freedom, achievement, contribution, creativity, adventures, travels, learning, and personal and spiritual development. They feel good that they do not need to ask for permission, to explain themselves, or to continually negotiate their plans. They also enjoy their own company and their relationships, with men as well as women, unrestrained by the boundaries of traditional role expectations. Several of them relish exceptional, joyful moments and relationships with people and do not seek consistency and reliability from specific people but in benevolent universal forces, which fulfil their needs.

14. What Do They Tend to Miss?

A sense of companionship when attending social functions or going on outings, holidays, or shopping trips is one of the things single women miss. While eating solo in restaurants or watching movies alone are options experimented with, the stories do bring out a sense of feeling different from the crowd and even the experience of discrimination in social spaces due to their being alone.

Sometimes, at a social function, people relate out of obligation or pity or ignore a single woman due to her being different. Also, in social conversations with married people, when children, husbands, and so on are the subject, there is a sense of disconnection and isolation. In such a context, it is difficult to share the different significant life experiences that a single woman holds. Often at parties, the men engage together in one room while their wives do the same in the kitchen, and so a single woman does not seem to belong anywhere. And there is a sense of awkwardness in the hosts also around how to treat a single woman. So they are thus sometimes not invited to parties.

Single women constantly face the challenge of how to not be emotionally vulnerable to dysfunctional relationships with men without losing their joy, softness, and warmth in life. They have to be vigilant, distinguishing between dysfunctional destructive male dependency and loving a human being. They miss the sense of ease and trust in relationships with men.

Another vulnerable aspect for single women is around sickness. The issue of whom they may fall back on when physically unwell arouses a concern which has been shared by several of the women. This creates dilemmas as well as difficulty in such situations as there is no taken-for-granted support system available. Asking for help and support is difficult and things do not come naturally, particularly if they live alone or are seen as strong. Single mothers, whether with biological or adopted children, carry an additional emotional and physical responsibility in bringing up the children.

The themes from the life journeys are not present in every single woman's story, nor do they happen all the time or in every interaction. Different women experience them in a variety of combinations. There is also some interconnectedness between some of the themes and they can augment the impact of each other. Interestingly, through the intersection and varied combinations of these themes, there are repeated patterns in the lives of single women in society creating similar overall experiences. Single women experience the themes in different combinations and intensity depending upon their stage of life. And the combinations impact emotional states and well-being differently.

The reason for highlighting these themes is not to say that the women have not found ways of dealing with them or of living life meaningfully and joyfully. I am bringing to awareness what single women have often encountered in their journeys and the paths they have created through their learnings.

*****

Epilogue:
Learnings and Vision for the Future:
A World Thriving with Diversity

Uma Jain

As I reflect upon the journeys of single women, including my own, I am in touch with the richness of learnings about what it means to navigate our lives. Through our storytelling, we share our learnings with others who grapple with the status of being different from the mainstream. We also offer our perspectives to create a better world for all of us.

We cannot change society and culture until all those who have a role in perpetuating the status quo acknowledge their part, find something in that change for themselves, and become willing to make shifts. I find several parts of the current social order – single women, men, married or partnered women, and society as a whole – to be partners in this major social transformation that needs to happen, and is already happening. I will now share how I see each part playing a role in the current state and what I envision happening in the decades to come.

Single Women

Many women have had access to education and models of living life different from the dominant narrative of society in the last several decades. While each of us as a single woman is finding our own unique path in the process of struggling with the often-unexplored terrain of our life, there are many milestones of personal development that several of us cross. I find some nuggets for a joyful, meaningful, and wholesome life as a single woman. These can stand us in good stead in our moments of struggle and aloneness. We can also show the way to men, women, and other people with social identities outside the dominant narratives of society, in their struggle and journey.

My pictures of emerging single women around the world as they learn and practise these learnings are:

- A woman with clarity of her values and living her values. She is willing to pay the price for making choices based on her cherished values as against making choices based on advice, expectations, norms, and fears. In her journey, she finds strength and support both from within and from others as she moves on with values-based choices.

- Even in the in the midst of contrary experiences, she retains her trust in self and in other human beings. The way to go she has discovered for herself is to look for exceptions even when the majority of people seem to disappoint. Special people are always there in the midst of the crowd.

- She practises empathy and forgiveness for her own well-being and does not write off people who disappoint her at a particular point of time. She has learnt to understand that they operate on what they know best and they themselves are on their own path of discovery. People may give both pleasant and unpleasant surprises.

- She enjoys moments, 'here and now,' with people she values and those who value her. The key to her being able to do this lies in not seeking role-based responses or permanence in relationships. She experiences the joy that is possible by being in the moment.

- As a single woman, she has come to accept that people who live a life different from the dominant narratives of society, more so than others, need to find their anchor within. The emerging single woman does not let others or society define who she is and what she becomes. She is crossing a significant milestone in her growth – accepting the possibility that she may not in her lifetime have the comfort of belonging to the mainstream. And she reminds herself that that has never been, and is not, her priority in life. She rejoices in being different, sees it as special rather than less or more. She creates and lives a rich and meaningful life in the long run.

- Reflecting, learning, and growing – these are the key to a single woman's life of joy and meaning. She cultivates her passions and interests – professional or hobbies. They are a great companion. They keep her alive, positive, and joyful. Self-care through a good diet and a fitness routine – physical and psychological – is a part of it. She is continually finding her gifts and her life's purpose. She contributes wholeheartedly to the people she is in contact with, and to society, with her talents and resources. She feels valued for who she is, irrespective of her marital status.

- Single women are connecting with other single women, asking for and giving support, and building a community of like-minded women.

- Single women across the world live with an awareness: we have, in our life, chosen to play a part at this point of time in the history of human kind, according to what we have the propensity for, are best prepared for, and are meant to play.

We feel alive, are enjoying our part and its outcomes with some detachment. We lead the path for change following our heart and embrace our destiny as it emerges. We see ourselves as instruments for change in the society which is happening but give up both the doer-ship for what is good in our life and a sense of victimhood for what does not feel good.

These are some scenarios I visualise of single women moving forward with their lives. I believe these journeys will be a catalyst for readers to visualise and create more models of living for single women and other non-dominant social identities.

Men

Based on my observations, conversations, and experiences in a variety of settings, I believe that the social change has been and will be challenging for men, though in different ways. The imperatives for men to shift are increasing faster and stronger but men's perspectives and stances are changing with much less speed, on the whole. There are some fairly repetitive patterns and processes – conscious or unconscious – related to men which I set out below. I must mention, though, that not all of this applies to all men; but I would like us to consider the possibility that some, much, or all of it could be applicable to many men.

I believe and would like to continue to believe that today's men are normally well-meaning and well-intentioned, as well as intellectually fairly progressive in their thinking. However, their repertoire for dealing with changing and emerging women is not expanding. They operate more often either from the usual repertoire of domination, consciously or unconsciously enjoying the unearned privileges that their social identity bestows on them, or get fearful, confused, or angry. They are not learning how to continue to feel powerful without being discriminating and oppressive.

I believe that many men find themselves on shifting sands. They feel shaken deep down, though they do not openly acknowledge it, even to themselves. They seem to be losing the confidence to relate to the emerging women and to deal with them as equals in work roles, as well as in personal relationships. They tend not to recognise or express their feelings but enact them often as a reaction to counter women voicing their feelings and experiences of inequity and injustice in social processes. They also tend to simplify the situation by pacifying, justifying, sarcasm, avoidance, and other such responses, rather than expressing their dilemmas. They believe that they are doing all the right things and would like to, and try to, convince themselves and women that this is the reality.

The question is: how long will this already-shaken social system keep supporting men in maintaining the status quo? The data of the journeys in this book is another wake-up call for men and my wish for them is that they will choose to heed it.

My dream and vision for men is as follows:

- Men across the globe are waking up to the reality that the privileges of patriarchy are not serving them well and will not protect them forever. Many men are feeling the push, desire, and freedom within themselves to accept this emerging reality and investing in their own all-round self-development.

- They are moving out of the shaken privileges, protective shield, and internalised gender roles of patriarchy as well as its prison. They are empowering themselves and shedding the handicaps created by male privilege and power.

- They are allowing themselves to experience and bring out their own personal potential as human beings in roles rather than being bound by gender stereotypes, images, and roles.

- Men are learning to own up and express feelings. They are growing and emerging as androgynous beings to build a more meaningful life and relationships – whether married or single. They are giving themselves the freedom to experience the richness of human emotions – the vulnerability, need for support, dependence, and need to nurture and care – and learning to express them in relationships.

- They take up roles in the family suited to their own preferences than the specified societal roles of earner, provider, protector, or 'the strong one,' even when contrary to their own feelings.

- They are making changes because they see something in it for themselves, not simply as a favour or act of patronage for women.

Partnered Women

Partnered women in my understanding play a role in the social dynamics around single women and they can be partners in the social change. Patriarchy, in its dysfunctional aspects, is perpetuated not only by men but by the conscious or unconscious collusion of women themselves. This collusion happens in several forms.

Married or partnered women many times accept and even propagate gendered roles due to their fears, convenience, or their own gendering, even when they are not really comfortable with them. This perpetuates the system.

The data from the journeys in this book reveals how they are often a party to the othering of single women and end up adding to the latter's experience of isolation. They offer advice to single women to marry or approve their single status due to their own sense of ambivalence towards their marriage, irrespective of how the single woman feels herself. Also, there are situations when, perhaps due to their own personal experience of the marriage that they are in, they fail to empathise with the single women and make them the subject of their envy and anger in personal as well as professional settings. My vision and invocation for partnered women is as follows:

- They are making choices in their lives, and fight their own battles with society, which makes them more at peace with themselves.

- They are choosing to operate on their strengths and courage in living the life of their choice.

- They use their privilege of belonging to the dominant identity not for othering and excluding, but to include single women in the social spaces.

- They are taking the courage to question and change the norms and traditions of patriarchy that are not viable in the current world. They collaborate in creating a fair, just, and supportive society for their own growth as well as for single women.

Society

The journeys in this book clearly highlight that, at one level, there are forces that have started the change, but simultaneously, there are forces that maintain the status quo of the dominant narrative of society. With their increasing emergence as professionals as well as androgynous human beings, some women need to choose to be single in order to have a life of freedom, dignity, and meaningfulness. More marriages are likely to break down if social norms and processes continue in this way. There could come a time when married women will be asked, "How come you are still married?" or "Why did you get married?" as opposed to single women being asked, "Why are you single?"

Society must take cognisance and ownership of its own responsibility in this phenomenon. It needs to re-examine patriarchal values and assumptions about the ideals for men and women, the roles in a family unit consciously or unconsciously being played out, and the costs for people who do not fit into traditional roles. Society needs to practise the values of inclusion, equity, and dignity for all. In the absence of this, the current trend seems irreversible.

What does the future hold? Will this continue to be the narrative of single women and the societal scenario for the next 20, 50, or even 100 years? I believe not. I feel the winds of change blowing. We are part of a major social change happening globally, though in slow and somewhat invisible ways. The journeys of single women in this book and of many more across the globe are a testimony to this. I visualise several changes at the societal level across cultures and geographies, in the coming decades.

- The age-old narrative of a woman's life – a woman with a man as a husband and biological children – is changing. Singlehood as a way of life is accepted without questions or judgements. Society respects the freedom of women to make choices about their life which work best for them. And it recognises that they are also serving some crucial social needs. It also acknowledges that there are many other models of living life already happening, and these are not being compared with or against the age-old dominant narrative.

- We have envisioned and are creating a society in which women have the chance of reaching their highest potential as human beings. They choose a way of life which gives them joy and meaning. At the same time, they do not have necessarily to struggle with a choice between 'family or career.'

- We have created a society in which there is inclusion and respect for all, no matter what marital status, sexual identity, or gender identity they choose, with no questions and doubts due to their being different. Such a society offers acceptance and has systems of care for all and has the benefit of the unique gifts of all.

Is this a good place to end? It does not seem like an end and it is not. It is the beginning of a newly constructed story of the lives of single women and of all human beings on the planet.

*****

About the Contributors[1]

Heather Berthoud, USA

Heather Berthoud lives in Takoma Park, MD, leading Berthoud Consulting, a trusted partner for leaders that encourages organisations to experience, understand, and self-direct enterprises that are life-affirming in their means and ends. She enjoys writing, yoga, hiking, and dance. She has been a faculty member for the American University Master's in Organization Development. She is a member of the NTL Institute and the Gestalt International Study Center, and a certified mindfulness meditation teacher.

Shobha Sarma, India

Shobha lives in Bengaluru. She has been single since her divorce, after a short married life. Shobha worked in housing finance and medical transcription for 20 years and retired voluntarily in 2011. She

---

1 The biographies of contributors with pseudonyms are not included

currently pursues her passions of doll making, crochet, and other crafts. Shobha loves to travel and take on any adventures that come her way. She believes in the philosophy of the Bhagavad Gita: do your duty without expectations.

Dr. S. Uma Devi, India

Uma Devi had an illustrious career as an economics professor. She has published books and many articles on economics, gender, and development. She has been a visiting fellow at the Centre for Care, University of California and the Centre for Women's Studies, Harvard University, and an external adviser to the ILO and UNO. Currently a Sanyasin (Hindu Nun), she lectures widely on Vedanta and pursues her passion for music.

Julian Walker, UK

Julian is currently a writer and facilitator, an associate of the equality and human rights consultancy Brap, UK, and a member of the NTL Institute, USA. As a civil servant, she has had stints as departmental speechwriter to home secretaries and as an independent governance consultant in Afghanistan, Bosnia, Libya, Palestine, and several other countries. As Director of Policy and Research for Barnardo's UK, she worked to promote race equality and diversity.

Deborah Howard, USA

Deborah Howard, esq., M.S.O.D., is the founder and president of Guiding Change Consulting. She is a leading organisational consultant and professional certified coach, having previously worked as a public interest lawyer. She brings intercultural insight and a passion for social justice to her work – helping leaders and their teams transform themselves and the world by tapping into their wisdom. An ex-board member of the NTL Institute, USA, she is an author of two books.

Archana Shrivastava, India

Archana has worked in the social development sector for over 20 years, focusing on transforming capacities of different groups and working on the rights of children, women, adolescents, youths, persons with disabilities, disaster victims, and more. Archana is an OD consultant, a trainer, a life coach, and a governing board member of several NGOs. A single adoptive mother, she loves tiny pleasures and strives to live in the moment. She enjoys music and relationships with diverse people.

Dr. Sharon Miller, USA

Sharon Miller was born in North India and spent her childhood on the Indian subcontinent. She received her Ph.D. in sociology from the University of Notre Dame and taught as well as did research until retiring in 2018. Currently she lives outside Seattle, Washington and spends her time gardening and hiking. Any chance she gets, she returns to the heart of her soul, India.

Rita Aggarwal, India

A gold medallist in psychology for her master's and bachelor's, Rita brings 35 years of experience in the field of psychology. With an independent clinic, Manodaya, in Nagpur, she became a pioneer in psychological counselling in Central India. She has been an all-India director for the Indus Entrepreneurs project for women entrepreneurs and a TEDx speaker. A regular columnist to a leading newspaper, *The Hitavada*, Rita is a human resources trainer.

Anjali Khanna, India

Anjali Khanna is the vice president of human resources with a prestigious group of educational institutions. She moved forward in her professional career after losing her husband at the age of 33, and brought up her daughter to become an interior architect. She conducts trainings and workshops in areas of her expertise, including emotional intelligence, the empowerment of women, sexual harassment, and more. She is an enthusiastic network builder and finds joy with friends.

Tangil Smith, USA

Tangil Smith, an SHRM-certified professional, is the CEO and executive director of DreaMakers L.L.C., founded in April 2008, focusing on providing career coaching and advisory services to varied groups. Tangil has worked in corporate America and influenced people as a coach, trainer, and advisor in the talent-intelligence space for three decades. She loves to bring people together for the common goal of helping others have a life of meaning and fulfilment.

Priya Vasudevan, India

Priya Vasudevan is an HR leader who straddles the world of strategy and execution with ease. She has led highly specialised organisation development initiatives, leadership development practices, and C-suite talent acquisition. Priya received a National Award in HRD and Training, 2014 from the Indian Society of Training & Development. She has published in respected international journals. Based in Mumbai, Priya also works for women's empowerment and past-life regression.

Dr. Mukta Kamplikar, India

Mukta Kamplikar founded MUKTA – Liberating Human Potential, a consulting firm, after working 20 years in various Indian and multinational organisations. As a consultant, she works with clients across India and the USA in the area of human capital development. A Ph.D. in marketing, Mukta has done post-doctoral research work through AMDISA. She has several publications on business and leadership. Mukta also paints passionately and has authored four poetry books.

About Dr. Uma Jain

A fellow of the Indian Institute of Management, Ahmedabad, Uma Jain has been a teacher of organisational behaviour at management institutes, a corporate human resources manager, an internal and external organisation development consultant, and an organisational leader over the last four decades. She has trained and consulted in varied areas of organisation development, values and culture building, leadership, group dynamics, and diversity and inclusion, widely in India and other countries, including the USA, Dubai, Austria, Singapore, and Mauritius. Uma Jain has made significant contributions to the field of applied behavioural science nationally and internationally in her various institutional roles including that of president, dean professional excellence, director of the organisation development certification programme at the Indian Society for Applied Behavioural Science, vice chair of the board at NTL Institute, USA, and director, Academy of HRD, Ahmedabad, India. She strengthened institutions as a leader and nurtured the competence of many professionals in various dimensions of human process dynamics as a facilitator.

Uma Jain has used her path-breaking models and insights as a trainer, consultant, and writer, with several papers and three books to her credit. Her book *Developing Leadership for the Global Era* won one of the best book awards from Delhi Management Association in 2006. Some of her papers are: 'Transcending Cultural Boundaries for Human and Organisation Development: Experiences of International Exchanges Between India and USA,' published in the *Handbook of Organisational Behaviour*, and 'Live Theatre of Conflicts in T-Groups: Actors, Audience and the Dramaturge,' illuminating the facilitation of gender dynamics in groups, in the journal *Perspektive Mediation*, Deuschland. In her writings, she brings a unique blend of conceptualisation along with data generated through experiential interventions.

As a single woman who has been carving out a new path for living her values and truth within her social context, Uma's passion for building a more sensitive society to diversity and gender issues led to her work with single women. This book uses personal narratives on the life journeys of single women, highlighting the terrain they have covered, to make society more aware and respectful of single women in particular and all non-dominant social identities in general. Based at Vadodara, India, Uma is deeply committed to personal evolution through behavioural science work, yoga, music, and spirituality.

*****

Printed in the USA
CPSIA information can be obtained
at www.ICGtesting.com
LVHW052006081223
766044LV00030B/1941